Mahaananda Reiki

The Influence of Tangible Consciousness

F.Lepine Publishing

ISBN 978-1-926659-37-4

Copyright © Cori Leach / SukhiDevi **2017**

Dedication and Acknowledgments

I dedicate this book with love and gratitude to Sigung Hasting Albo and MahaVajra for the blessings of their teachings, guidance and support; and also in loving memory to Simon Lacouline, who transformed my rough sketches into the Mahaananda Reiki logo and who continues to inspire me.

Gratitude to my editors, Mahaananda Reiki Master Teacher Richela Chapman and Melissa Bird; to my hand position model Mahaananda Reiki Master Teacher Rachel Heller; to my photographer Leah Wayne and photograph editor Xenia Besora Sala; and to Laura Mariana Avila for the cover art. To my friends and students who encourage me and help me in so many ways, thank you.

Table of Contents

INTRODUCTION 7

MAHAANANDA REIKI LEVEL I

LEVEL I SPIRITUAL TECHNIQUES 13
- Meditation Techniques 15
- Emotional Integration 17
- The 21 Masks of the Ego 20
- Japa Meditation 27
- Simple Mantras of Great Power 31
- The Five Elements of Creation 37

LEVEL I REIKI 43
- Introduction to Reiki 44
- Energy and the Chakra System 49
- Initiation and Lineage 55
- Evaluation and Treatment 63
- Hand Positions and Treatment 67
- How to Use Spiritual Techniques for Yourself When Doing Therapy 81
- The Five Precepts 82

MAHAANANDA REIKI LEVEL II

LEVEL II SPIRITUAL TECHNIQUES 85
- The First Two Siddhis 87
- Transmigration 90
- The Peaceful Soul 95
- The Well-Being Mantras 96
- Esoteric Symbol Empowerment 103
- Chakras, Soul and Evolution 117

LEVEL II REIKI 119
ABOUT REIKI LEVEL II 121
THE REIKI SYMBOLS 121
HOW TO DO A REIKI TREATMENT USING SYMBOLS AND MANTRAS 131
THE PHYSICAL AND EMOTIONAL/EXPERIENTIAL ASSOCIATIONS OF CHAKRAS 139
INFUSING INANIMATE OBJECTS WITH REIKI 146
ADDITIONAL TECHNIQUES 148

MAHAANANDA REIKI MASTER LEVEL

MASTER LEVEL SPIRITUAL TECHNIQUES 155
KAMACHAKRA 157
THE UNBREAKABLE GAZE 161
DIVINE AND UNIVERSAL CONSCIOUSNESS OF THE CHAKRA 166
MAHAANANDA MANTRA 168
THE VAJRA STATE OF BEING 169
MASTERING COMPASSION 173
THE FAVORABLE MANTRA 176
DIVINE MOTHER / VISHWASHAKTI 177
CONSCIOUSNESS OF USUI SENSEI 178

MASTER LEVEL REIKI 179
FOURTH REIKI SYMBOL—DAI KO MYO 181
ADDITIONAL TECHNIQUES 182

CONCLUSION 185

REFERENCES 186

Introduction

The Goal of Mahaananda Reiki

I created Mahaananda Reiki as a guide to inspire all levels of Reiki-ists to enhance their transformational power by incorporating effective spiritual techniques. The Reiki sections take the beginner step by step through experiencing energy and understanding lineage, initiation, hand positions, symbols, and Reiki techniques. Both beginners and Masters can embrace the sections on Spiritual Techniques as continuing education for elevating sensitivity to both the tangible and intangible nature of the world; then to embody the spiritual power available to influence that nature.

Mahaananda vs. Traditional Reiki

What distinguishes Mahaananda Reiki from traditional styles of Reiki?

Perception of the Transforming Essence—The Mahaananda tradition acknowledges the transforming essence of Reiki to be consciousness as well as physical energy—they are one and the same, as Chi is tangible consciousness. Our state of being, the resonance of the symbols and our own consciousness affect the state of being of another.

Therapy Technique—Traditionally, Reiki therapy doesn't involve the therapist beyond putting ourselves in the proper mindset and intuitively affecting the chakras with our hands, but we are mostly a simple compassionate conduit of universal life force energy. In Mahaananda Reiki, we also incorporate transformation from the Soul level, purposely affecting the consciousness of our client with our own consciousness. We transmigrate into the other, aware of being One, and add prayer in the form of Sanskrit mantras.

Chakras—Traditional Reiki training focuses on hand positions without delving deeply into the consciousness of chakras Mahaananda Reiki embraces chakra consciousness as an integral component of therapy.

Spiritual Experience—Almost every Reiki lineage includes some level of spiritual experience for the mastership certification. In *all levels* of Mahaananda Reiki, training in ego purification and states of being is essential for the practice as it brings higher consciousness and understanding of suffering. Mahaananda Reiki also includes training in esoteric mage techniques to further empower the Reiki symbols.

As in other styles of Reiki, the Mahaananda Reiki-ist strives for non-attachment to the outcome of the treatment, leaving the result in the hands of God, or Karma.

The Mahaananda Reiki Levels

The Level I Spiritual Techniques section concentrates on your personal growth with basic meditation, using mantras, understanding and purifying our friend the ego, and with awareness of the spiritual components of the natural world from the perspective of the Five Elements. Level I Reiki explains Reiki, energy pathways, chakras, Reiki initiation, the Mahaananda lineage, how to practice feeling energy, and demonstrates basic hand positions.

The Level II Spiritual Techniques section demonstrates how to "go inside" your client, teaches mantras for specific types of therapy, explains how you can super-charge the Reiki symbols using an esoteric Japanese technique, and explores chakras from the level of soul. Level II Reiki presents the first three Reiki symbols and how to use them for in-person and distant therapy and for infusing Reiki energy into inanimate objects, as well as additional Reiki techniques. This section also includes practical guidance on how to incorporate the Level I and II consciousness concepts into your therapy sessions.

The Level III Spiritual Techniques section addresses how to master desire, how to enhance the focus and power of your attention, how to experience the universal consciousness of chakras, how to know yourself as human, soul and divine, the consciousness of Truth, how to foster the attitude of a compassionate servant, how to practice self-containment, and how to give a favorable blessing to finish up your therapy session. Level III Reiki teaches the master symbol and advanced techniques.

Mahaananda Reiki Initiations

Contact me at sukhi@desertlotusreikiandmeditation.com or the ShaktMa organization at info@shaktima.org for information on online initiations.

The Mahaananda Logo

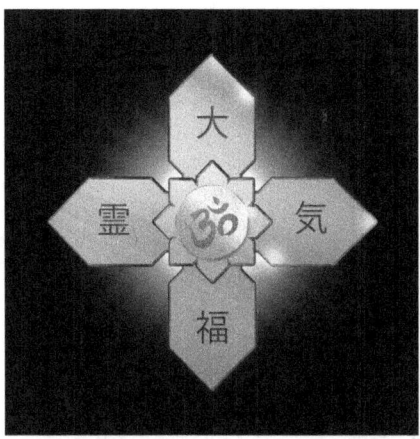

(You can find the color version of the logo at www.desertlotusreikiandmeditation.com)

The Mahaananda logo expresses the spiritual nature of the therapist and the therapeutic techniques:

- the Hindu Om symbol at the center represents the vibration of the universe
- the 8-petaled lotus is the Buddhist dharma wheel
- the cross: as a stylized Christian cross it reflects the power of faith; as a double vajra it represents the five elements and the four directions—the foundation of the physical world. The double vajra is also a symbol of protection
- the kanji for Mahaananda Reiki embody the arms of the cross
    - 大 "Maha", meaning Great
    - 福 "Ananda", meaning Bliss
    - 霊 "Rei", meaning Spiritual
    - 気 "Ki", meaning Nature
- the luminous green hue represents compassion
- the glow from within the logo shows the consciousness of the therapist affecting the world

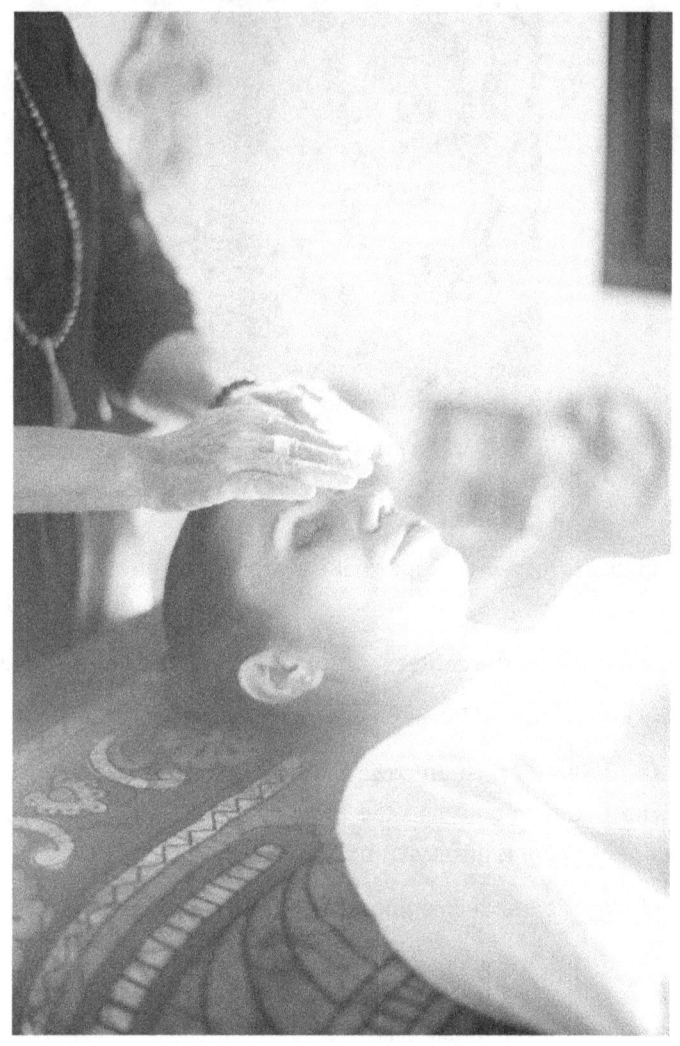

(You can find the color version of this photo at www.desertlotusreikiandmeditation.com)

This photo captures the supernatural radiance of the Heart chakra. It was taken with no artificial lighting; and the only source of natural light was a window directly behind the Reiki therapist.

Mahaananda Reiki Level I

Level I Spiritual Techniques

Meditation Techniques

What is Meditation?

Lots of people think they can't meditate because they believe it means sitting with absolutely no thoughts, but that is the most difficult and advanced form of meditation. The secret to meditation is not to have *no* thoughts; it's to be at peace even when there *are* thoughts.

My definition of meditation is paying attention to something in order to alter my state of being, or state of consciousness. You can pay attention to the feel of your breath, to your emotions, to the meaning of a mantra, to nature, or a variety of other things. The goal is to allow your spiritual consciousness to override your human identity for a few moments. Next are simple steps for the most basic meditation. It's most effective when you practice in a silent environment.

Four Basic Meditation Steps:

1. Sit and breathe, paying attention to your breath.
2. Pay attention to yourself, inside.
3. Calm and clear your mind. Each time you realize that your mind has wandered to thoughts, gently bring it back and do your best to not judge yourself.
4. Observe that you are aware of yourself. This is Self-awareness, or Consciousness.

The first step is to sit, relax, and pay attention inside. Most of us aren't used to paying attention to the same thing for more than a few seconds. If there is no change—if there doesn't seem to be movement, sounds or variations—our mind will try to pay attention to something else because it really likes to be stimulated. When you notice that your mind is wandering, softly bring your attention back inside. It's not an active pushing away of the thoughts; it's simply choosing to manage what you look at. Also, it's easier to bring your mind back, and keep it back if you have a disinterested attitude toward your thoughts. It's like you are looking at a blue sky and very much enjoying the richness of the color, and birds fly across your view—you simply keep your attention on the sky. Or if you are driving in the rain, you of course pay attention to the road ahead rather than the windshield wipers.

At this point you might have an additional goal in your meditation such as contemplation, or sinking into states of being. If you want to contemplate a spiritual philosophy for deeper understanding and possible revelation, review what you want to contemplate, do the four basic meditation steps, and simply *allow* information to come. If you actively think about it, your intellectual mind might filter or alter the Truth. This is a good way to contemplate the consciousness of the Reiki symbols or the meaning of the VishwaChakra. Another way is to softly and slowly repeat a mantra (a phrase to bring a state of being) along with the contemplation. You will use this technique when contemplating the first two Siddhis (see the section on Siddhis). These are examples of passive meditation.

Meditation can also be more active in nature. Japa is a type of meditation in which you use a prayer necklace called a "mala" to count while chanting mantras and contemplating (see the section on Japa). An example of this would be meditating on the Five Elements.

Transcending

Sometimes during meditation, you might "transcend"—it seems as if you fall asleep, but your spiritual experience is simply overwhelming your human experience. You don't lose consciousness; rather it is more of an awakening of your consciousness.

With practice, you will gradually be able to remain aware at the same time you go into expanded states of consciousness—this is known as *conscious* transcendence. You have a foot firmly in both worlds, and even though you might feel rather zoned out, or in another world, you are able to perform simple tasks such as going for a walk or cooking. When you fully return to your normal state, you will remember at least part of what happened spiritually during this transcendental experience.

Conscious transcendence reminds me of waking up suddenly from a deep sleep and rising to start the day—my mind is still absorbed in the images of my recent dream while I put on the coffee.

Emotional Integration

Emotional Integration is a way of taking responsibility for your own happiness. It's a meditation that helps you learn how to get out of drama—how to stop holding on to knee-jerk emotional reactions that don't feel good. And with regular practice, you will experience conscious responses to life experiences, rather than having dramatic reactions in the first place.

Here's an example of obvious internal drama. I saw a movie just the other day about a young man who received a much smaller share of a family inheritance than his brothers and sisters did. He became so angry, feeling like a victim, and hated his siblings until the day he died. Did his life change from one day (the day before the will was read) to the next (the day after the will was read)? No, everything was the same except for his reaction to the destruction of his expectation.

Sometimes our internal drama is hidden. We are taught from a young age to repress our painful emotions with words like "suck it up" or "big girls don't cry". So we stuff our emotions down deep inside us so no one will see them. But no one told us to pay attention to them later. This is like hiding your dirty smelly socks in a drawer where, over time, the smell becomes worse and worse. Many self-help gurus teach you to focus on the positive and do things that you enjoy—it works, but it's only a temporary distraction and that hidden sock odor flavors the way you respond to life in both obvious and subtle ways. With this technique, you turn away from your happy distractions just for a few moments and take your dirty socks out of the drawer and smell them on purpose. You face the pain of your emotions so you can do some powerful self-healing.

Learning this technique immediately changed my life, so I share it with anyone open to learning. My first Reiki Master teacher Sigung Hasting Albo (Sigung) lost his life as the result of a car accident in 2008. He was my martial arts master, my Reiki master, a spiritual teacher to many and my friend—I so loved this wonderful man! I was still grieving eight months later when I attended my first seminar with my current spiritual master MahaVajra (Maha). Maha taught emotional integration, which allowed me remember Sigung with happiness and gratitude, rather than with pain and grief. And I did it with one 3-hour session (as the small print on advertisements says, "Results may not be typical"). Integration on other subjects has taken me much longer. Resolving a heartbreak from the end of a love relationship took over a year, but most integrations have taken less time. (You can find more about Sigung and Maha in the Lineage section of this book.)

This meditation is a four-step process:

1. BREATHE (pay attention to your body)

   Simply breathe. Pay attention to the feel of your body breathing; maybe the feel of the air moving through your nose, or the rise and fall of your chest.

2. INHABIT—Pay Attention Inside (pay attention to your emotions)

   Become aware of your emotional suffering—it might be very intense or just a slight distraction. Look for an uncomfortable or even painful physical sensation at the base of the throat (Throat chakra), the center of the chest (Heart chakra), or between the bottom of the rib cage and the belly button (Solar Plexus chakra). Breathe in the experience.

3. FEEL (allow yourself to hurt)

   Be vulnerable and sit in the pain, surrendering to feel it as deeply as you can. Do your best to not resist it, and to not distract yourself from feeling it. Allow yourself to sink in and have that internal temper tantrum, or feel sorry for yourself. It's normal that your mind might want to think about something else, or try to find solutions to the problem, or even try to convince you that it's silly to do this. But this meditation is all about emotions, not thoughts. So when you notice you are thinking, gently bring your attention back to your emotions and breathe the pain.

4. OBSERVE (separate yourself from your pain)

   You are not your emotions, you *observe* your emotions. Observe the physical feel of the suffering in your Throat, Heart, or Solar Plexus chakra, and breathe. The part of you that observes is not in drama or suffering, it is simply gazing while in a state of compassion. You are just observing what's inside the drawer (those smelly socks), like watching a movie or an ant crawling along the sidewalk.

Continue to breathe, feel, and observe. The drama (or physical pain) of your emotion will begin to subside, and eventually dissolve. YOU ARE DISSOLVING RESISTANCE TO EXPERIENCES THAT BRING EVOLUTION (OR TO THE WILL OF GOD, OR KARMA). As you go through the process, you might remember other events when you felt the same emotion. Jot them down and then work on these experiences another time.

If after 30 minutes or so your suffering has not dissolved, end your meditation and move on to the "happiness" step. Try to not be discouraged—for some intense experiences it's like moving a mountain one teaspoon at a time.

Generate Happiness! *(for no reason)*

Finish up your meditation by forcing yourself to be happy! This is pure happiness that you create just because you want it; it's not dependent on outside experiences. Imagine that all the cells of your body become smiley faces. Your Heart chakra, in the middle of your chest, is a giant smiley face. All of your blood cells are smiley faces. They are so happy! They vibrate, jumping up and down with joy. They flow through you and up and out of your Crown chakra, creating a fountain of happy faces that swirls around your body. Force yourself to smile! Laugh out loud! Put your arms around yourself and hug yourself.

Following Up

<u>Integrating Past Events</u>—Later, integrate other events with the same emotion attached to them—the ones you remembered during the current session. We learn from our earliest moments of life to have particular emotional responses to events—what's normal in our family or culture, and what gets us lots of attention. As you integrate all your emotions through related events you break this conditioning. The next time a similar event occurs, you don't attach as much drama to it and you don't respond the same way.

<u>The Power of Paying Attention</u>—Even if you are not able to do integration at the very moment you feel an emotional reaction, paying attention inside all day long (exhaustive observation) is a powerful habit. Every time you notice you are not aware of what's going on inside you, gently bring your attention back. I measure the spiritual success of my days by how long it takes me to bring my attention from the outside event or "cause" of my emotional reaction back inside in order to continue observing.

DOING THE EMOTIONAL INTEGRATION TECHNIQUE WILL NOT TURN YOU INTO AN EMOTIONLESS ROBOT! YOU WILL ALWAYS FEEL, BUT YOU CAN *CHOOSE* TO FEEL HAPPY AND *MAKE IT HAPPEN* BY INTEGRATING YOUR EMOTIONS.

The 21 Masks of the Ego

The 21 Masks of the Ego is a tool to help you understand why you hurt; which in turn helps your emotional integration become more efficient. The masks play a part in happiness and in suffering for both yourself and others. This visual summary of the masks is a good quick reference.

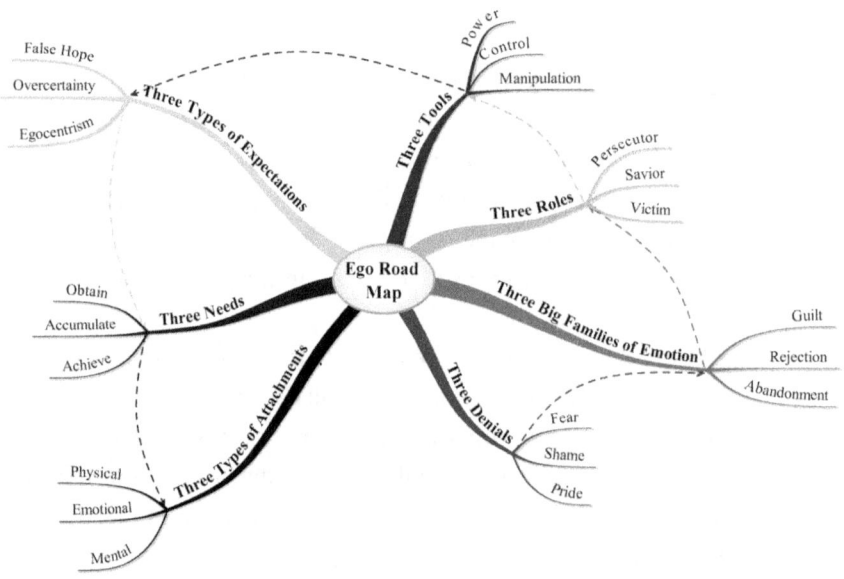

(You can find the color version of the Ego Road Map at www.desertlotusreikiandmeditation.com.)

These emotions and behaviors aren't inherently "bad"—sometimes they are just the way we take care of ourselves and others. When emotions are related to your own internal goals and you don't project them outside to others, they are usually helpful to you. For example, internal pride because I bettered myself in some way through achievement is really nice, but if my pride leads me to play the persecutor by talking down to someone who didn't achieve that goal, my behavior causes suffering.

Your purpose in this study is to try to understand how the 21 Masks play a part in happiness and in suffering for both yourself and others. Remember, happiness is a choice you can make.

The Three Denials

The denials of Fear, Pride and Shame prevent you from being aware of yourself, so that you don't understand your emotions.

Fear is avoidance—it's a technique to keep you safe. Fear is a God-given gift to stay physically alive, making you instinctively afraid to step into oncoming traffic or to touch fire. But sometimes when you feel emotional fear, it prevents you from taking a chance or making a change in yourself. For example:

- You didn't ask a cute girl for a date because you didn't want to experience being turned down
- You didn't apply for a job, because you were afraid to find out you weren't good enough

Pride is a lie that protects your image to both yourself others—it is the attitude of being right. You justify your mistakes. You pretend you are perfect. You want to feel important so you say or do things to compete or get attention. When this pride is very intense, not feeling important or not being "right" can generate self-hatred, leading to shame. For example:

- Your boss didn't remind you to finish that project
- You don't deserve to be treated that way

Shame is feeling unlovable—you don't feel "good enough". Society teaches what is beautiful and valuable—some cultures find perfection in thin-ness, while others see wealth and abundance in a big body. It's normal to compare yourself to those standards. You may prefer spending time alone, not wanting to expose yourself to the negative attention of judgment, or to the possibility that no one would even notice you. Some examples of the negative self-talk of shame are:

- I'm not beautiful enough
- I'm not young enough
- I'm not smart enough

The Three Emotions

Our emotions fall into three primary categories—Abandonment, Rejection and Guilt.

Abandonment is when someone is not available to you—they went away, or were never there at all, and you feel very alone. You can feel abandonment when someone or something leaves you, or when *you* are the one that leaves. For example:

- A teacher dies
- Your relationship with a lover or friend ends
- You grow up without knowing your father
- You lose something you need or value (you left your job, or your car was stolen)

Rejection is when someone or something doesn't treat you in a way that makes you feel loved--someone could love you, but not in the way *you define* as love. When you feel ashamed of yourself, that is self-rejection. For example:

- Your husband gave you a vacuum cleaner instead of roses for your anniversary
- You were cut off in traffic
- You were served by a rude waiter

Guilt depends on your *perception* of whether or not others approve of what you did (or failed to do). If you did the "right" thing but others judge you, you feel guilty. If you do something "wrong" but others praise you, you don't feel guilty. For example:

- In middle school, I scored 100% on a test which skewed the bell curve for other students, and they blamed me for their lower scores—I felt guilty
- A gang member committed a crime as part of his gang initiation, and his homies had a celebration in his honor—he didn't feel guilty

The Three Roles

The roles of Persecutor, Savior and Victim are behaviors used to soothe the suffering felt from the three emotions.

The Persecutor applies force that hurts others (their victims)—mostly as an attempt to soothe his own feelings of rejection or self-rejection. Even angry thoughts are a form of persecution. For example:

- Your boss was inflexible with your vacation approvals because you didn't make her feel respected
- A bully tries to make others "respect" him to cover his own lack of self-worth.

The Savior wants to help decrease the suffering of others, but also wants to receive something (love) in return. The reward could be outside attention and/or an internal feeling of worthiness. Saviors usually view the people they help as "victims" of persecution that need saving. Sometimes it hurts the savior so much to see the suffering of others that she wants to fix the situation to soothe her *own* pain. (See the discussion on Compassionate Servant in the Reiki Master section.) Examples are:

- You feel shame when a Reiki client is disappointed with the results of your treatment
- Without being asked, you did some distant Reiki for a friend's sick mother; you later told your friend about it, partially in order to receive her gratitude

The Victim feels persecuted by someone (or by life) and doesn't deserve it. Usually, she makes sure someone knows about it in order to get attention and care, and to confirm that she is "right". Victims can also play the role of persecutor by complaining. Sometimes the savior also feels like a victim. For example:

- A lonely mother tells her friends that her grown son never calls her anymore
- Facebook posts complaining about politicians who don't care about the people is a statement from the point of view of both victim and persecutor
- You might hear a savior lamenting "I have too many people to take care of, I'm so tired!"

The Three Tools

We use Power, Control and Manipulation to apply force in order to influence the actions or attitudes of others—for selfish or for helpful reasons.

Power is a single act of strong expression—it can feel violent at some level. For example:
- An unhappy customer makes a public scene and insists that a clerk be fired
- A parent gives a 4-year-old child a quick swat to persuade him to stop playing in the street

Control means applying continuous force in a systemized way. Control can help you be aware and responsible. For example:

- A woman denies sex to her boyfriend whenever he watches the game with his friends instead of taking her out to dinner
- A late payment penalty helps you remember to pay rent on time each month

Manipulation applies force in a sneaky, subtle manner which often misrepresents the truth. Manipulation commonly invokes a sense of false urgency, guilt or expectation in others. For example:

- You loan your car to a desperate friend who needs it to get to work and keep his job (he doesn't tell you he has another offer, but likes your car better)
- A nerdy honor student writes a research paper requested by a flirtatious beautiful girl
- You lure a friend to their surprise birthday party by asking for help on a household project

The Three Expectations

The expectations of False Hope, Overcertainty and Egocentrism are focused on the results of specific circumstances—different from the virtues of Hope and Faith, which express a universal feeling that everything will always be fine.

False Hope is a fantasy, believing that something impossible will happen. For example:

- Your belief that if you lose weight, everything in your life—your love life, your job, your health—will be perfect, and you will finally be happy (without working on personal growth)
- When my sons were 5 or 6 years old, they absolutely knew that they would grow up to be Power Rangers. Of course, this wasn't possible, but as part of the fantasy they learned to value being kind, being brave, working as a team, and taking care of others

Overcertainty has no doubts. You believe you have total control and everything will turn out well *without you needing to be prudent or wise* (or turn out badly *even if you are prudent or wise*). In overcertainty, you take things for granted. For example:

- You'll pass the class without studying for the final exam—or even you *won't* pass the exam no matter how much you study
- Your lover will never leave you (or your lover will never stay)

Egocentrism is greedy, thinking "it's all about me!" We don't care about the welfare of others and don't think about the karma created by our actions. Children are naturally egocentric, but usually become more compassionate as they are grow and experience the consequences of their behavior. For example:

- Someone at the grocery store with an overflowing basket rushes and pushes to get in line ahead of another shopper that has only a few items
- Musical chairs is a game that celebrates egocentrism

The Three Needs

The needs are the expressions of getting something for yourself by Obtaining, Accumulating, or Achieving. If others are happy and their needs are filled, it is good to fill your own needs while practicing non-attachment (see The Three Attachments below).

<u>Obtaining</u> means acquiring something you need or want. Usually It is related to a physical object, such as purchasing groceries or a pair of shoes. It could cause suffering if you aren't prudent in prioritizing your purchases, or you make a purchase in order to avoid your fear of non-conformity (the self-rejection you might impose on yourself if you don't feel "cool"). For example:

- You just bought the latest iPhone only because you want to fit in with your friends
- If you bought a new pair of shoes instead of buying groceries, there would be no dinner for the family

<u>Accumulating</u> is obtaining more and more resources when you have enough. Accumulation causes suffering when it's driven by the feeling of dis-satisfaction rather than satisfaction or contentment. For example:

- Saving for retirement is responsible and makes you happy when your state of being is prudence, but you're not happy if you are saving because of fear.
- You have way more pairs of shoes than you need, since you really only wear about five of them

<u>Achieving</u> means reaching a goal or objective. It causes suffering when it is motivated by self-infatuation or by jealous competition. For example:

- You were looking for the feeling of achievement when you earned your college degree—you received status (competition), and also useful job skills
- Personal growth authors write books in order to help others—they also gain recognition for themselves
- Practicing martial arts helps you get in shape—and have fun emulating Jet Li. Or it could be used to become a more powerful bully.

The Three Attachments

The three types of attachments are Physical, Emotional and Mental—they are people, things or experiences you are fond of and very much want to have in your life. It hurts when you lose things you are attached to. Even when you have someone in your arms, or something in your hands, you can suffer as you imagine a future time when you no longer have them. The solution to this pain is non-attachment, which means to enjoy something when you have it, accepting that everything is impermanent. You can be responsible in doing what needs to be done to keep the objects of your attachment in your life; and at the same time be willing to let them go.

Physical Attachments are mostly related to possessions, and can grow from necessity or sentimentality. For example:

- Your home, your altar, and your car are necessary for your well-being (you work on becoming unattached from your car, but you still make your car payment)
- A dear friend of mine suffered a lot when she lost her wedding ring

Emotional Attachments are mostly related to relationships—with your spouse or lover, your children, your friends and coworkers. Relationships don't even have to be with real people. For example:

- Your heart can be broken when your lover leaves you
- You suffered so much when your teenage children hated you during their "hormone years"
- You mourned your favorite TV show being canceled because you miss the characters

Mental Attachments are mostly related to achievements and to your sense of identity (who and what you identify yourself with), and are very much tied to pride—wanting to be right, or loved. For example:

- You felt ashamed when you failed a test in school
- You voted the straight Democratic ticket without researching the candidates or issues
- Your normally good-natured dad angrily turns off the TV when the Cowboys are losing

These masks of the ego are simply expressions of your powerful need to feel loved. The goal of understanding yourself with this wisdom is not self-judgment, but non-judgment; it is to learn how to become happy.

First, become aware of how much you look for love outside of yourself and the self-suffering you cause by doing so. Next, observe yourself and forgive yourself. Then you can finally release your attachments to that illusion of outside love and can look *inside* for love—the source of true and unshakeable happiness.

Japa Meditation

A powerful way to raise the consciousness of a mantra inside yourself ("charging a mantra") is to do Japa. Japa refers to chanting a mantra, usually 108 times, while using the mala (a string of beads) to track the number of recitations you've done. It's a way to count without paying much attention to the counting, so you can focus on the philosophy and visualization of the mantras.

This consciousness is already inside of you—you are made of it—but the charging process increases your awareness of it so you can use it. As the consciousness becomes more available it naturally brings personal evolution, and you can also use it along with Reiki therapy.

What is a Mantra?

A mantra is one word or a series of words, such as a prayer, which help you sink into a spiritual experience. To live the consciousness of a mantra, contemplate its meaning while reciting it. You may say the mantra out loud, whisper it, or think it silently. Saying it aloud brings the consciousness into the body a bit more because you are affected by the physical resonance of the sound of speech. Recite the mantra at any speed that feels comfortable. However, if you choose a very fast pace make sure the words are fully pronounced and recognizable so that they resonate well in consciousness.

Mahaananda Reiki teachings include Sanskrit mantras rather than English mantras because in Sanskrit each letter has its own meaning. Therefore, every word, in addition to its dictionary definition, has many layers of vibration in consciousness and creates the most powerful influence on your state of being. I'll give an example of this concept in the word "deha". The dictionary definition is "body", but looking at the letters we find something like "presence of form, and the expression of that wisdom". Very deep and rich, isn't it? Also, if you were to chant mantras in English, you would be using words that you say every day in a common, non-sacred attitude—making it easier for you to remain in your normal daily human experience rather than sinking into a conscious state of being, which is your goal. And if you use Sanskrit *only when you are in a sacred practice*, then the moment you begin saying a Sanskrit mantra the mind connects to the deep conscious state of being—the Self.

What is a Mala and How Do I Use It?

The mala is a string of beads used when reciting mantras, or prayers, similar to a Catholic rosary. The most common mala is a 108-bead necklace. Usually one larger bead (known as the guru bead) connects a tassel to the mala. This guru bead represents bindu, which is the point of Consciousness from which the universe originates. Malas can also be made with fewer beads in the form of a bracelet.

Bead Material and Size

Beads are made from seeds, wood, bone or stone. Seeds (such as rudraksha or lotus) produce life. Wood allows life to flow, but is more structured than seeds. Bone is more dense than wood, and also supports life in a structural way. Stone doesn't support biological life—it consists of raw energy and strong building materials. So, seed represents life force and is very good for therapists; stone represents structure, building and strength and is excellent for any type of mage work or other ritual practice; and wood and bone are in between. General users typically prefer wood as it represents both structure and life, and is the least expensive.

Bead size is based on your personal preference. Depending on the size of your fingers, the bead size can influence how easy it is (or not) to shift the beads. Smaller beads aren't as noticeable if you are wearing your mala under your clothing. The guru bead is usually a bit larger than the other mala beads, or offset from the other beads (a bit outside the circle of beads)—it makes it easy for your fingers to feel when you've completed 108 recitations of the mantra.

The Tassel

The tassel also helps your fingers feel when you've completed your 108 mantra recitations. Since it is connected to the guru bead (bindu), it expresses "energy that flows from consciousness". At the end of each mala, touch the tassel to the 3rd Eye to show your intent to embody the consciousness.

Mala Technique

Hold the mala with both hands, creating a loose loop. Position your hands with palms up, letting the mala rest on either the ring or major (middle) fingers. Place your right thumb on the first bead *after* the guru bead (the guru bead will be closer to your body). Shift the beads by pulling the mala toward you with your thumb, one bead per each recitation of the mantra. Don't use your index finger to shift the beads, as this will empty the charge that creates the power item—see below. That first bead after the guru bead will be "1", and the guru bead will be the spacer after the 108th bead. The guru bead isn't counted.

Guidelines for Charging Mantras—The 9 x 12 Formula

To "do one mala" means to repeat a mantra 108 times using your mala. The most commonly recommended formula for charging mantras is 9 malas per day for 12 consecutive days. If you aren't using a mala, repeat the mantra for about 35 to 45 minutes, depending on the length of the mantra or how comfortable you are pronouncing it. If you want to do more than 9 malas per day, it's best to charge several different mantras. Perform all nine malas of one mantra, and then nine malas of the next mantra (such as 9 malas of Peace, then 9 malas of Compassion). If you miss a day, try to do one mala on that day to hold the energy, and then add a day at the end of the 12 days. If you miss two or more days, start the process over because you lost the higher level of consciousness that daily practice creates.

Using a Mala as a Power Item

When you are doing Japa, the consciousness of the mantra permeates your mala and transforms it into a power item. Then when you wear it while doing Reiki therapy it elevates your energy. You can observe tangible evidence that a charged mala holds consciousness by holding your hands together in a prayer position with your mala in between them—first wind the mala up in a compact bundle so it fits snugly between your hands. You can feel a subtle vibration in the mala. When teaching this class in person, I offer my students to try it with my mala, and every one of them has felt the vibration.

If for any reason you get a new mala, you'll want to charge it with the mantras you already charged on your previous mala. For each mantra that you already completely charged, you only need to do one day's worth of charging on the new mala. For a mantra you charged with the 9 x 12 formula, do 9 malas in one sitting and the new mala is charged.

When you want to use the power for yourself, loop your mala several times and wear it on your left wrist. If it's for therapy, wear it on your right wrist—the energy that flows through your hand resonates with the charge. This difference in the use of right and left hands comes from the wisdom that the right side of your body is more Yang in nature (giving, or flowing out) and the left side is more Yin in nature (receiving, flowing in). You can also wear it around the neck for either purpose.

About the Mantra Teachings Which Follow

ॐ "Om". In the mantra presentations that follow I use the very simple definition of "universal syllable"; Om *is* simple, but also exquisitely beautiful and immense. Om was the first vibration in the world, and represents the pervasion of God throughout every manifested and potential possibility. Every Sanskrit prayer begins with "Om".

You will find the mantra pronunciation in the center column of the explanations; the italicized syllable has the accent. For example:

Sanskrit Word	Pronunciation	Meaning
Shanti	"*shahn*-tee"	Peace

Simple Mantras of Great Power

These well-known mantras are simple, and also some of the most powerful mantras in existence. They will return you to your original, pure, intended state—peaceful, compassionate, and powerful.

The best way to charge each of these mantras is with the 9 x 12 formula while contemplating the teaching. Begin each meditation session by breathing, paying attention inside yourself, calming your mind, and observing that you are aware of yourself. You can charge these mantras in any order you want, except for this guideline: charge the Three Suns only *after* you have completed all 12 days of both Peace and Compassion.

Remember to contemplate the meaning of each mantra while reciting it. You may say the mantra out loud, whisper it, or think it silently. Saying a mantra aloud brings the consciousness into the body a bit more because you are affected by the physical resonance of the sound of speech.

The Mantra of Peace

This soft mantra settles and clears your mind. The general meaning is divine Peace, Peace, Peace.

"Om Shanti Shanti Shanti"

Om	"ohm"	Universal syllable
Shanti	"*shahn*-tee"	Peace

Peace is much more than being peaceful amidst the trials of life, or the calm within the storm. The concept of Peace is the *absence* of conflict. Transform your perception so that you no longer perceive drama; if you let go of your judgments, you'll find that nothing is "wrong"—things are just happening. Contemplating Shanti brings harmony with life.

Visualize a clear blue sky while chanting this mantra. Try doing one mala of Peace before each of your other meditation practices to "get in the zone" (except for practices which make you very sleepy).

The Mantra of Compassion

This mantra soothes your emotional heart. The general meaning is divine jewel of consciousness; or, it is precious to be aware of what you experience inside yourself.

"Om Mani Padme Hum"

Om	"ohm"	Universal syllable
Mani	"*mah*-nee"	Jewel, precious and beautiful
Padme	"*pahd*-meh"	Lotus (symbol of consciousness)
Hum	"hoom"	Experience

I grew up associating Compassion with pity and with wanting to do something to end the suffering of the people I felt sorry for. But pity is agreeing with and supporting the drama of others.

From a spiritual point of view Compassion is deep understanding, and this understanding of yourself and others comes as you live experiences and practice at gently observing your responses to those experiences. *You can stop taking things personally.* In Compassion, you accept both happiness and suffering—whatever life brings you. First you observe, then you understand, and then you can choose to perform acts of loving kindness.

The Three Suns Mantra

This mantra raises your energy level and empowers your body. The sun is a source of energy and life. The three suns in this meditation are one sun perceived at three different chakras—these chakras represent the levels of divine, soul and nature inside you.

"Om Vajra Agni"

Om	"ohm"	Universal syllable (divine)
Vajra	"*vahdj*-ruh"	Diamond, lightning bolt (soul)
Agni	"*ahg*-nee"	Fire (nature)

<u>First sun:</u> Start by visualizing a radiant sun in your 3rd Eye—the middle of the forehead. Recite the mantra "Om" in your mind every few seconds. The most powerful level of Divine energy in the universe resonates with the mantra OM. Breathe.

<u>Second sun:</u> Next, visualize a radiant sun in your Solar Plexus—between the bottom of your rib cage and your belly button. The vajra represents the Soul, or what is indestructible like a diamond, and powerful and ungraspable like a lightning bolt. Recite "Vajra" in your mind every few seconds, aware of the most powerful energy source at the level of Soul. Breathe.

<u>Third sun:</u> Now, visualize that radiant sun in your Base chakra—at the base of the body between the sexual organs and anus. The most powerful energy force in nature is fire. Recite "Agni" silently every few moments. Breathe.

Taking your time, invoke the first sun in your 3rd Eye, the second in the Solar Plexus, and the third in the Base chakra all at the same time. They fill you up, radiating inside and outside of you. Feel the power at the Divine, Soul and Nature (or human) levels. Every cell in your body is experiencing Om Vajra Agni, feeling the power. Perform your japa while doing your best to keep the visualization going.

Because of the powerful nature of this mantra, it's best to charge it only *after you have completely finished charging both the Peace and Compassion mantras* to ensure that it won't provoke some small level of irritation in you. Also, don't charge this mantra while you are feeling disturbed or angry, because it could make you *more* disturbed or angry. And finally, if you charge this just before bed, your high energy level might make it difficult to fall asleep.

First Mantra of Atma Yoga

Atma Yoga is the "Yoga of the Soul". This mantra brings you to consciously exist *as* your Soul; it also affects the state of being of your body and mind.

"Aham Nivedin Aham Atma"

I am aware that I am Soul, or I am conscious that I am made of consciousness.

Aham	"ah-*hahm*"	I am
Nivedin	"*nih*-veh-deen"	Deeply aware of
Atma	"*aht*-mah"	Soul

Nivedin is both the highest level of pure thought (no expectation and no attachment), and a very tangible understanding of wisdom—divine level thought resonating in your cells and throughout your entire body. Contemplate that your body is not made of tangible matter. Contemplate that your body, your life force energy, your emotions and your thoughts are all made of consciousness. Your body feels tangible because it is consciousness holding its position and keeping its properties, but you are made of Self at every level. You are soul, living the experience of a human life.

It is wonderful to fall asleep each night while thinking or saying this mantra to yourself, because you drift inside to a deeper Soul state when you sleep.

First Mantra of Immortality

This Taoist mantra brings long life. It is also known as the mantra of the three living forces—mind, heart and body.

"Ni Na Ra Ra Hum Ra"

Ni	"nee"	Highest level of thought in nature
Na	"nah"	Presence in nature
Ra	"rah"	Powerful activation
Hum	"hoom"	Experience

Contemplate the consciousness that you are. You are the most noble, divine experience of nature; you are also very present in your body, the densest experience of nature. Your human existence is the temple of a divine being. The 3 "ra"s activate this experience in the mind, heart and body.

- All the resources of nature are available to your mind—bringing infinite creativity and clear thinking
- All the resources of nature are available to your heart—bringing infinite love, affection, and tenderness
- All the resources of nature are available to your body—bringing infinite life force and willpower; every cell pulsates with life and resources

Feel joy for abundance and infinite potential, and complete satisfaction with all that you have.

The Five Elements of Creation

The Svetasvatara Upanishad, part of the sacred literature of Hinduism dating around 300 BCE, explains that the universe was created out of emptiness in the form of five elements—earth, water, fire, air and akasha (space or heaven).

God created the world in the form of Love, or supreme consciousness, or universal substance. You can perceive this Love from five points of view, which are the five elements. It's like looking into your living room from a window, a doorway, or the ceiling—it's the same room but the view is a bit different. All of the elements exist at the same time in everything, everywhere, and the innumerable ways they flow and dance together create the variations in the universal substance that manifest as the variety of life—both physical things and experiences. The five elements of creation are not the physical elements you can see and touch; they are the spiritual *potential* for everything created. The properties, or consciousness of the elements are similar to what you experience in the physical elements, but not exactly, because it is all filtered through your human perception.

Through these meditations your awareness of and familiarity of with the five elements inside you and everywhere around you will grow much stronger. Eventually you can influence natural forces in the form of life events and therapy—this is manifestation. Just remember that manifestation abilities are limited by expectations and attachments (see an explanation of attachments in the section on the 21 Masks of the Ego).

All of the elemental mantras include placing attention on Hindu deities. The Heaven, Water and Air mantras also include Buddhist and Christian versions—you only need to charge one version, whichever is your preference. It is not required to be Hindu, Buddhist or Christian, or to feel you are praying to deities while you chant the mantras. You are simply invoking a state of being, or viewpoint of consciousness.

Use the 9x12 formula to charge the elements. Begin by breathing, paying attention inside, calming the mind, and observing that you are aware of yourself. Then meditate on each element while chanting the mantra. It is important to charge them in the order in which they appear here as each is a foundation for the ones which follow. You can charge more than one at a time if you like, but keep the proper order. For example, if you want to charge Earth and Fire during the same 12 days, you would chant 9 malas of Earth, then 9 malas of Fire each day. The associated chakras (see the section on Energy and the Chakra System) are included for those of you who are interested; paying attention to the chakras is not required for this meditation.

Earth

The general meaning of the Earth mantra is "Earthly nature of the Goddess Earth". Chanting this mantra invokes the divine nature of planet Earth or Mother Nature.

"Om Prithividhatu Bhumideviya"

Om	"ohm"	Universal syllable
Prithivi	"*pri*-tee-vee"	Earth (dirt)
Dhatu	"dah-*too*"	Properties of something
Bhumi	"*boo*-mee"	Earth (the planet)
Deviya	"deh-*vee*-yuh"	Referring to a goddess (Devi)

The properties of generation (or creation) and steadfastness prevail in the earth element, along with protection and abundance. Earth allows the essence of things to coagulate; it establishes the building blocks of structure. Contemplating earth, you can feel movement that happens over thousands of years, like an incredibly slow-motion wave of water. There is steadfastness and peace in the movement. The steadfastness allows progression without influence from the outside—this sustains intention and provides protection. (Earth also creates a magnetic field of protection against energy vampires. Energy vampires are people who haven't learned to find radiance and self-love inside themselves, so they are drawn to *and drain* the radiance of others). The abundance comes from the continual regeneration. The feeling of Earth is clean and pure.

Fire

The general meaning of the Fire mantra is "Powerful nature of Fire". This mantra invokes the divine nature of the Goddess Agni.

"Om Tejasdhatu Agnaya"

Om	"ohm"	Universal syllable
Tejas	"*teh*-zhahs"	Fiery energy or brilliance
Dhatu	"dah-*too*"	Properties of something
Agnaya	"ahg-*nie*-yuh"	Referring to Goddess Agni

The consciousness of Fire is radiation, transformation and purification. The light of God radiates and influences everything at every level; this radiance is both the cause and the result of transformation. Fire purifies, not by destroying something, but by transforming and elevating it to a higher nature. When a thing physically burns, it goes back to its most pure, simple divine state (like a complex tree being transformed to ashes). Every cell of a living thing, and every particle of matter inherently yearns to elevate and be one again with God—this constant change and elevation underlies the impermanence of this world, the inevitable evolution. You can see this in the movement of the flame—it never stands completely still, and it is never in the same exact shape.

Heaven

The general meaning of the Heaven mantra is "Oh, heavenly nature of Lord Shiva". Shiva represents the interaction between God the Creator and His Creation, similar to Avalokiteshwara in the Buddhist tradition and the Holy Ghost in the Christian tradition. (It's only required to charge one of these versions, not all three.)

"Om Akashadhatu Shivaya" (Hindu version)
"Om Akashadhatu Avalokiteshwaraya" (Buddhist version)
"Om Akashadhatu BhagavAtmaya" (Christian version)

Om	"ohm"	Universal syllable
Akasha	"ah-*kah*-shah"	Heaven; spiritual realms
Dhatu	"dah-*too*"	Properties of something
Shivaya	"shi-*vie*-yuh"	Referring to Lord Shiva
Avalokiteshwaraya	"ah-vah-loh-kee-teh-shwah-*rie*-yuh"	Referring to Avalokiteshwara
BhagavAtmaya	"bah-gahf-aht-*mie*-yuh"	Referring to the Holy Ghost

The Heaven element is also called Spirit, Self, Void, or Non-mind. Heaven is the pure space in which the will of God or karma (the process of elevating consciousness) is invoked in your life; it's where everything happens inside you and everywhere. It exists in the space between atoms, and throughout the entire universe. And Shiva (or Avalokiteshwar or BhagavAtma) is what provokes things to happen—what provokes experiences for your evolution.

The Heaven mantra holds a wonderful optional bonus. After charging it with the 9x12 formula, chant one mala per day for one year and an angel will accompany you for eternity. Yes, really ☺

Water

The general meaning of the Water mantra is "Oh, watery nature of Divine Mother". This mantra invokes the consciousness of Divine Mother.

"Om Apsadhatu Durgaya" (Hindu version)
"Om Apsadhatu Taraya" (Buddhist version)
"Om Apsadhatu Mariaya" (Christian version)

Om	"ohm"	Universal syllable
Apsa	"*ahp*-sah"	Water
Dhatu	"dah-*too*"	Properties of something
Durgaya	"duhr-*gie*-yuh"	Referring to Durga
Taraya	"tah-*rie*-yuh"	Referring to Tara
Mariaya	"mah-ree-*ie*-yuh"	Referring to Mother Mary/Maria

Water expresses the feminine aspect of God. Divine Mother supports, nurtures and cares for you—all of existence is cared for and bathes in the womb of Divine Mother. The softness of water cools and soothes you. The fluidity, or flowing movement of Water signifies non-attachment; everything flows according to the will of God and change creates less drama and pain.

Air

The general meaning of the Air mantra is "Oh, airy nature of the son of Hanuman", and invokes the concept of pure mind. The meaning of mind here is both the mind and the heart—thoughts and emotions.

"Om Vayudhatu Hanumantaya" (Hindu version)
"Om Vayudhatu Bodhicittaya" (Buddhist version)
"Om Vayudhatu CittAmalaya" (Christian version)

Om	"ohm"	Universal syllable
Vayu	"*vie*-yoo"	Air or wind
Dhatu	"dah-*too*"	Properties of something
Hanumantaya	"hah-noo-mahn-*tie*-yuh"	Referring to Hanumanta
Bodhicittaya	"boh-dee-chee-*tie*-yuh"	Referring to perfected mind
CittAmalaya	"cheet-ah-mah-*lie*-yuh"	Referring to pure mind

The consciousness of air expresses pure mind, communication, harmony and balance—it is the concept of non-resistance. Air is the element with the least tangibility, so substance in any form moves easily through it. Information in the form of vibration flows or vibrates easily through air. Light waves and sound waves and odor move through air more rapidly and with less distortion than through water or earth.

A pure mind allows you to think and communicate with focus and clarity (like Hanumanta, son of Hanuman the Monkey King). The air mantra opens your mind and other senses to a broader perception of the universe so you can be available to revelations.

Level I Reiki

Introduction to Reiki

The Meaning of Reiki

Reiki (pronounced "ray key") is a Japanese word which means spiritual (rei) nature (ki), although it's more commonly referred to as universal life force energy. It also refers to a system of spiritual or energy therapy performed by the transmission of ki into the body through the practitioner's palms ("ki" is the Japanese version of the more familiar Chinese word "chi").

Rei: 霊 Spirit

Ki: 気 Mind / heart / nature

The Spiritual Nature

When I first saw Vincent van Gogh's "The Starry Night" as a teenager, it immediately became one of my favorite paintings. Much later, when I was working as an accounting director, I had a poster of it framed for my office. Learning about energy in martial arts, in Reiki therapy, and in spiritual evolution helped me understand why I was so drawn to it—I could see the spiritual nature in the brush strokes.

(You can find the color version of "The Starry Night" at www.desertlotusreikiandmeditation.com.)

The spiritual nature (or universal life force energy, or consciousness) makes up, flows through, and connects all things, both "living" and "non-living". Imagine this energy as the ocean, and our bodies as fishing nets in that ocean. There is no containment of water within the net, and no separation of the water inside one fishing net from the water outside that fishing net. Neither is there separation of the water in that fishing net from the water in the next fishing net. Now imagine a few small fish in the net. Even though the net is filled with water and the fish are composed mainly of water (or space, at a deeper level), the fish need a fresh flow of water constantly moving through the net to stay in perfect health. The flowing water brings nutrients and oxygen to the fish, and also removes the toxic waste naturally created by the metabolism of the fish. The removal of toxins is the concept most applicable to Reiki.

Now compare one of these nets to your body, and these fish to the cells of your body. Your body and cells need a constant flow of energy from the universe around you to flush out the dis-ease created by the emotional and mental stress that results naturally from living your daily life.

Since we are made of this spiritual energy (or tangible consciousness), it's more difficult for me to understand why we appear to each other to be so solid and separate from each other than to imagine that we are not. Simon Lacouline, in his book "Broaden Your Perception", expresses this concept beautifully. *"How can atoms almost entirely made-up of nothing...be the raw stuff that makes up the solid matter that surrounds us? How can we then touch and grasp objects? Why can't we walk right through walls? How can a floor support your feet if the matter of which it is composed is made up of emptiness?"* This thought explores the non-concept of space. And in the non-concept of time we can describe a simple object (such as a table) as energy with a memory, standing still. When you imagine removing the human perception of time, you can see the table as being a seed, flowing into a tree, flowing into a piece of lumber, flowing into a table, flowing into rotten wood, flowing into ashes, flowing into the earth, flowing into a seed, and so on, all at the same point in time of "now". When you peek through the veil of time and space, you can understand the true nature of Reiki therapy.

Reiki and How It Works

From the moment of conception, energy (chi or Ki) flows into and resonates through our bodies (or we wouldn't be alive) flushing out the effects of stress such as anxiety or illness or pain. But sometimes the stress effect is so intense that it clogs up the flushing system. The energy flow can become unbalanced or even blocked in the affected areas of the body, and then we don't feel well. Reiki therapy can help restore the energy flow.

Reiki therapy is the most natural and simple thing in the world. When your stomach hurts, you naturally hold your hands over your abdomen. Parents know what to do if their child falls down and skins her knee—they put their hand on it. Energy flows through the hands and into the stomach or the knee, and it begins to feel better. That's Reiki, just without the technical training or the initiation (see the section on Initiation).

During a treatment, the Reiki therapist inserts him/herself as a middle-person in this energy flow process. The body of the client is drawing energy from the universe, but it flows first through the Reiki therapist before entering the body. As the energy flows through the therapist, the frequency increases, creating an intensity that flushes the energetic system and effectively clears and balances the energy pathways. Reiki therapists do not impose an external influence or therapy on the client—we merely assist our clients with their own self-healing process.

You could think of the stressed energetic system as a house that has been closed up for a few weeks while a family is away on vacation. The Reiki therapist is merely opening up the windows and doors, allowing a cool breeze to flow through and refresh the stagnant air.

Or imagine that energy is water. Visualize a rain gutter, after a storm, clogged up with leaves, twigs and dirt—this is a stressed energy pathway. It begins to rain again, and the raindrops fall on the roof of a house, and flow naturally to the gutter. But the water isn't able to enter the clogged gutter; it just flows over it and down to the ground below. Even if a little of the rainwater does seep into the gutter, it doesn't flow freely, but works its way little by little around the leaves, forming little stagnant pools. The Reiki therapist will clear the gutter by using a garden hose. The hose itself is the body of the therapist, made into a powerful conduit by the initiation. The therapist naturally opens the garden faucet and directs a forceful stream of water that clears the clogs by placing his/her hands over the chakras with intent and compassion (see the section on Energy and the Chakra System).

Stress itself isn't a bad thing; it's what makes us move. The sound of a baby's cry creates a stress in her mother—the maternal instinct—to care for her baby. Hunger is stress in the stomach reminding you to eat and nourish your body. When the alarm goes off in the morning, the stress of feeling responsible makes you get up and get ready for work. It's the *effects* of long-term stress that hurt. However, emotional integration and contemplating the 21 Masks of the Ego can help you resolve the *causes* of stress, and Reiki helps resolve the *effects* of stress.

General Purpose and Benefits

The purpose of a Reiki treatment, using physical terminology, is to clear and balance the energy pathways of the body. The natural, strong flow of ki (or chi) both relaxes and animates your body, promoting the self-healing process. Spiritually speaking, Reiki influences the vibration of consciousness by helping to relax your resistance to evolutionary experiences. The most basic benefit is stress reduction, which naturally soothes lots and lots of ailments. Good results are common with mild depression, anxiety, headaches, migraines, pain, asthma, unrestful sleep, grief, PMS, poor mental focus, and many more conditions. Reiki accelerates recovery from illness and surgeries, and also helps ease the transition from life to death.

Traditional Western Medicine and Reiki

Reiki facilitates (it does not replace) traditional Western medicine. Reiki and Western medicine work very well together. There are nurses, chiropractors, massage therapists, veterinarians, doctors and hospitals that provide Reiki along with other treatment programs. If you counsel a client to stop taking their medications and use only natural or holistic methods you are opening yourself to a lawsuit. My preference is to first try various forms of natural therapy, such as Reiki, mantras, herbs and food—but use common sense.

When my children were little and got a sore throat, I tried Reiki, vitamins and soup. If that didn't work, we went to the doctor's office. When I get a urinary tract infection, I try cranberry juice, water, Reiki and mantras—sometimes it works and sometimes I end up taking antibiotics. Reiki is very effective with surgery—used prior to and just after surgery it relaxes the body so that it works *with* the surgery rather than resisting the invasive violence. Reiki also speeds up the physical recovery process and reduces the pain. Someone with severe depression could begin to use Reiki while gradually reducing the dosage of their prescribed medication to the minimum required—<u>but this should absolutely be done under a doctor's supervision.</u>

Spirituality and Science

Reiki is spiritual in nature, but not affiliated with or contrary to any specific religion. Religion is a man-made structure, customized to various cultures and belief systems, which provides a vehicle that helps us connect to God and live well in society. In my mind, religion seeks to answer three questions—where do I come from, what is my purpose here on earth, and what happens to me after my body dies? These are really just one question: "What is my relationship to God?" Reiki doesn't seek to answer these questions. It merely acknowledges the spiritual nature of everything and the natural ability we all have to use it in order to influence physical and emotional health.

Of course, there are various opinions about this. The US Conference of Catholic Bishops in 2009 warned Roman Catholics to avoid Reiki because it lacks scientific credibility and is dangerous to Christian spiritual health. The bishops stated that the "laying on of hands" by a trained Reiki master clashes with Christian belief. A beloved Baptist member of my own family agrees with this idea, doing his best to convince me that only God can heal, and that any other intangible form of therapy must come from the Devil. This view is not limited to Christians—I also know several Buddhists that feel the practice of Reiki goes against their beliefs. On the other hand, I know of three nuns and many Buddhists in my hometown that are Reiki practitioners. Google Reiki and Religion, there are lots of articles to read, pro and con. You must make up your own mind about this.

As far as scientific credibility, there is not yet a means based on the scientific method to measure the beneficial effects of Reiki, even though the benefits are becoming acknowledged by Western medicine hospitals. TV's famous cardiovascular surgeon, Dr. Oz, invited Reiki practitioners into his operating room to treat patients during open heart surgeries and heart transplant operations, commenting that "Reiki has become a sought-after healing art among patients and mainstream medical professionals."

The US Army is observing the effects of "integrative therapies" with programs which include Reiki, acupuncture, art therapy, bio and neurofeedback, medical massage, meditation, Qigong and yoga as treatment for soldiers who have been diagnosed with Post-Traumatic Stress Disorder (PTSD). I had the honor and wonderful experience of working at one of these clinics, the R&R Center at Ft. Bliss Texas, for four years.

Reiki is Only for Good

Prospective students have asked me if there is a dark side to Reiki—can we invoke or influence negative energies? To me that's like asking if pure clean air or clean water has a dark side. All energy (tangible consciousness) is made of Love, and what we call "negative energy" is the suffering of emotion which comes from attachment and expectation (see the section on the 21 Masks of the Ego). Reiki influences physical relaxation, which influences emotional relaxation. Reiki energy is inherently good and nourishing and there is no possible negative purpose or effect.

Energy and the Chakra System

In this first level of Reiki, I speak about chakras primarily from the physical energy viewpoint. I'll speak about chakras being the resonance of consciousness, and the association of chakras to physical and emotional/experiential aspects in the Reiki II section, and about the chakra as universal movement in the Master section.

Chakras are Formed by the Movement of Energy Pathways (Nadis)

The Sanskrit term nadi comes from the root "nad", meaning "motion". A nadi is a current in the vital or astral body along which the prana (vital force) and information resonates. These are the energy pathways in our bodies. Various ancient sources tell us that there are between 72,000 and 350,000 nadis—energy rides the breath, rides the blood, and flows along other pathways as well. Sushumna, Ida, and Pingala are the primary nadis.

Sushumna (meaning most gracious) is also known as the Central Channel and extends along the spinal column from the Base chakra to the Crown chakra. The Ida (also known as Chandra, or Moon nadi) resonates alongside the right of Sushumna, and Pingala (also known as Surya, or Sun nadi) resonates alongside the left. The common ancient teaching expresses that Ida and Pingala first meet Sushumna Nadi at the Base Chakra, then wind back and forth, continuing to intersect with Sushumna to form a vortex which becomes each major Chakra, until they meet and end at Ajna (3rd Eye) Chakra. This was the experience of the first holy people who recorded it, and how most images depict it.

7 Major Chakras with
Sushumna, Ida and Pingala

Location of the Chakras

The Sanskrit word "chakra" means "constantly turning" or "perpetual motion", and it is this vortex movement that draws energy into and through our bodies. The major chakras are the areas where energy most powerfully enters the body and where we physically feel it most intensely. "Intensely" is a comparative word because most people feel the energy as very subtle. A Reiki treatment focuses primarily on the major chakras because it is efficient to work where most of the energy is flowing.

The eight major chakras are aligned in an ascending column from the base of the spine to the top of the head. The most widely accepted interpretation recognizes seven chakras by considering 3rd Eye and Jade Gate to be the front and back of the same chakra. However, the experiences associated with each are quite different so Mahaananda Reiki recognizes eight.

The various names, locations and associated colors of the major chakras and the Dan-Tian are listed below. I always use the first (and most common) name in the list, but please get familiar with all of them so you can avoid the experience I had back in 2006—I was so excited to finally meet some other Reiki masters in my area...but during our first conversation, I didn't know what "2nd chakra" meant, so of course they thought I was a Reiki "poser" and a fraud; it was embarrassing and they didn't want to be my Reiki friends. The New Age practice of associating colors of the rainbow with chakras represents the range of energy frequencies from the lowest frequency at the Base chakra to the highest frequency at the Crown—most physical at the Base to most spiritual at the Crown. Many people experience different patterns of color when giving or receiving energy treatments.

- Base chakra (or Root, Muladhara or 1st chakra) is located just inside the perineum (the soft area between the sexual organs and the anus), and is represented by the color red.

- Sacral chakra (or Hara, Svadhishthana, Navel or 2nd chakra) is located a few inches below the navel and is represented by the color orange.

- The Dan-Tian is an energy center, not an actual chakra, which encompasses the entire digestive system in the abdomen; the center is located at the navel. Most Reiki traditions include a hand position at the navel.

- Solar Plexus chakra (or Manipura or 3rd chakra) is located between the bottom of the rib cage and the navel, and is represented by the color yellow.

- Heart chakra (or Anahata or 4th chakra) is located at the level of the physical heart but in the center of the chest, and is represented by the color green.

- Throat chakra (or Vishuddha or 5th chakra) is located at the base of the throat, and is represented by a medium blue color.

- Third Eye (or Ajna or 6th chakra) is located at the center of the forehead, and is represented by the color indigo (blackish-blue).

- Crown chakra (or Sahasrara or 7th chakra) is located about 4 inches above the top of the head, and is represented by the colors purple and white.

- Jade Gate chakra (or 8th) chakra is located on the back of the head at the occipital ridge (the pointy bone near the base of the skull), and is represented by the color green, which transitions to black in its center.

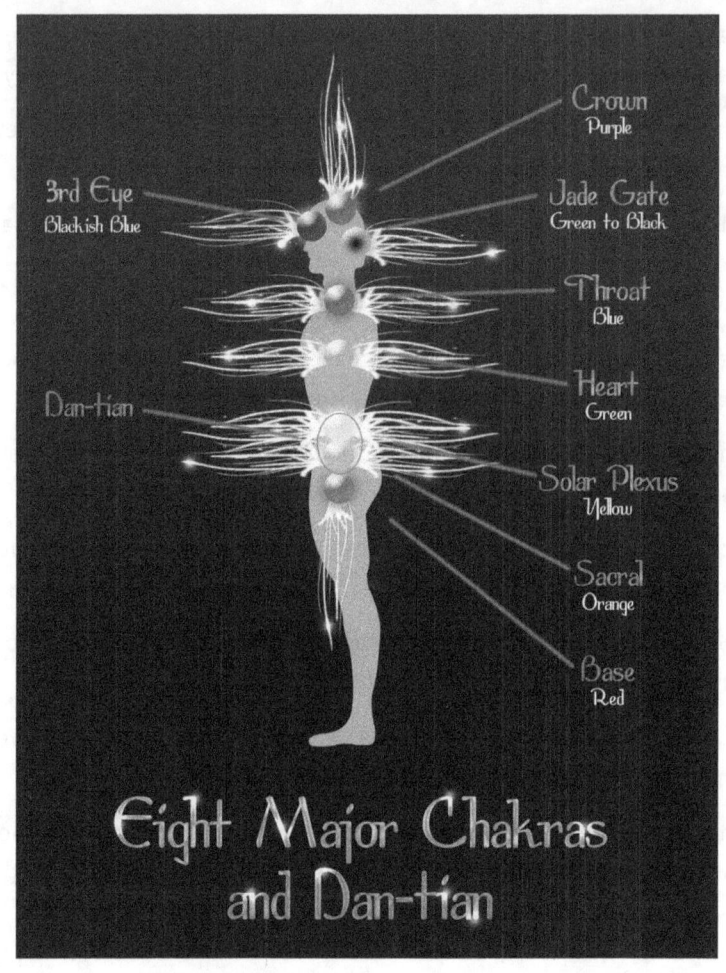

(You can find the color version of "Eight Major Chakras and Dan-Tian" at www.desertlotusreikiandmeditation.com.)

Important minor chakras turn at all of the major joints as well as the palms and the soles of the feet.

Location of Important Minor Chakras

- Shoulders
- Elbows
- Wrists
- Hips
- Knees
- Ankles

- Lao Gong (palm)
- Yong Quan (sole of the foot)

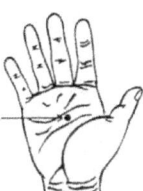 

Sigung referred to chakras as "energy gates". There's one more gate located between the shoulder blades that both of my masters taught about (see the Lineage section). Sigung called it the Yang Diamond. He would hug each student after class, pressing both of his hands there to give Reiki. Maha calls it the Host chakra and describes it as the area where the soul enters the body—this is the origin of the egg-shaped aura that surrounds the body and is sometimes seen as angel wings.

Another important physical and spiritual point in the body is the pineal gland (so named because its shape resembles a pine cone). This very small endocrine gland (about the size of a grain of rice) produces melatonin, which modulates sleep-wake patterns. Although situated deep within the brain, brain surgeons have encountered that it is sensitive to light and therefore it is associated with spiritual perception.

Initiation and Lineage

What is Initiation

Initiation (also referred to in other traditions as empowerment or attunement) is a spiritual practice in which a Master pushes a consciousness and/or skill to his student. This consciousness has been shared many times from person to person over thousands of years, beginning with the original Master who received a certain wisdom or power by revelation. Sometimes the consciousness received acts as a catalyst which allows spiritual seekers to raise their own consciousness more quickly as they do their practice. An example of this would be an initiation for a mantra. Other times it raises the consciousness of the seeker to such a state that a new skill or power is immediately evident and available. This is the case with the Reiki initiation.

The Master gives initiation for each level of Reiki training—Reiki I, Reiki II, and Reiki Master/Teacher. Some traditions consider the Master and Teacher levels as one combined level (Level III), and others separate them to two levels (Level III and IV).

Reiki Lineage Begins with Usui Sensei

Reiki lineage is a documentation of the series of Master Teacher initiations in each tradition, beginning with Usui Sensei—the original Master of modern Reiki—through the most recent student.

Usui Sensei

The Reiki wisdom was revealed to Japanese Buddhist monk Mikao Usui (Usui Sensei) as an enlightenment experience in the 1920s. Sensei means "teacher" in Japanese. He had been on a 10-year quest to recover the secrets of spiritual well-being referred to in Buddhist sutras—common skills which had become esoteric thousands of years ago. He traveled to many Buddhist monasteries searching unsuccessfully for information, and finally surrendered to meditation and fasting at Mount Kurama. After 21 days Usui Sensei allowed a ball of light to strike and enter his 3rd Eye, and he lost consciousness. When he awoke he knew the four Reiki symbols—both their meaning and how to use them in healing. Usui Sensei conveyed this system to between 16 and 19 Reiki Master students (depending on the reference source) using initiation and oral teachings.

Mahaananda Reiki Lineage

The lineage chart below reflects the series of initiations (or flow of consciousness) that began with Usui Sensei and resulted in my own initiations. I received the Master Teacher initiation from both Sigung Hasting Albo and MahaVajra (see the following sections on Martial Arts Lineage and Clerical Lineage).

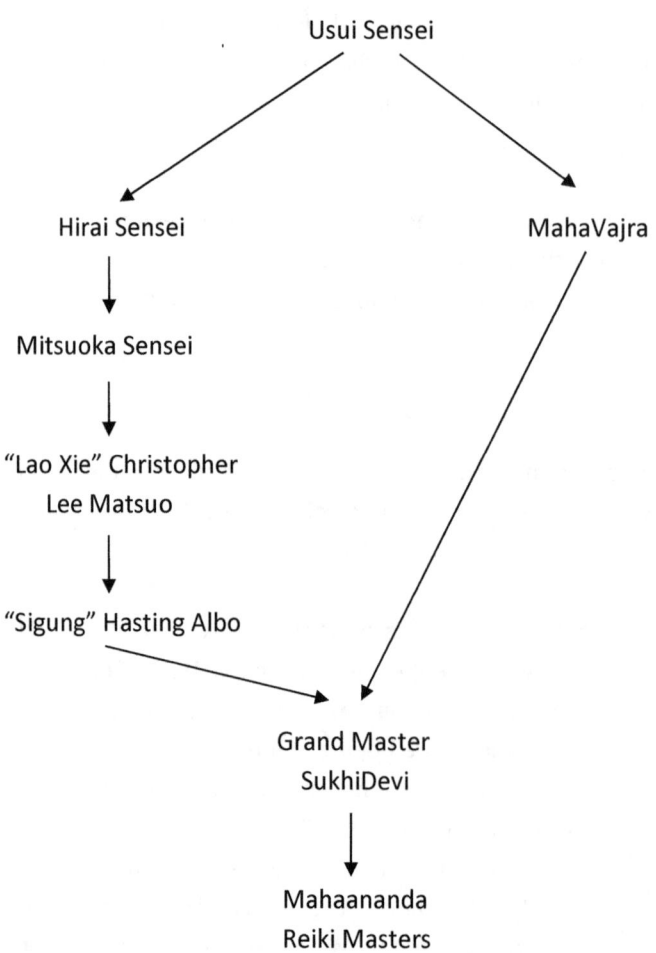

Martial Arts Lineage

Sigung, Sukhi and Lao Xie 2007

The entire lineage of Sigung Hasting Albo, master of Xen Martial Arts and Healing Arts Academy, is in the martial and natural therapy arts. My martial arts lineage began with Hirai Sensei, who was the last person to receive initiation directly from Usui Sensei—he was still in his mother's womb when she received her Master initiation. While giving Reiki, white light emanated from his mother's fingertips and white smoke or mist emanated from Hirai Sensei's palms.

Hasting K Albo ("Sigung", a title which means grand teacher) was Filipino by heritage, and born and raised in Hawaii. Sigung's grandfather Grandpa Albo was a skilled martial artist. His mother forbade Grandpa Albo to teach Sigung about fighting when he was small, so instead he taught Sigung martial arts "dances" and later showed him what they really were. Sigung shared the wisdom with his friend Christopher Lee Matsuo ("Lao Xie", a title generally used for a highly respected teacher. It translates as "old person". Lao rhymes with "cow" and Xie is pronounced "sher" as in Sherman).

After high school, Lao Xie became a martial arts and Reiki Master student of Hidetoshi Mitsuoka in Hilo, Hawaii—Mitsuoka Sensei had received initiation in Japan by Hirai Sensei. Lao Xie shared what he learned with Sigung and initiated him as a Reiki Master. Lao Xie now runs Dragon Gate Sanctuary in Honolulu, where he does therapy using the techniques of acupuncture, Tibetan Bon Shamanism and Reiki, and is a highly respected martial arts master.

Sigung started his own martial arts school in Hawaii, and in 1998 followed a girl to El Paso Texas. That relationship didn't last, but he stayed and began teaching, and eventually founded Xen Martial Arts and Healing Arts Academy. It was then that he met and married his beloved Simo (meaning wife of the teacher).

I was drawn to this school as a Kung Fu student after seeing Sigung perform at local martial arts tournaments in which I was participating. Since I didn't want to fight he assigned me to the Master Class, which was an advanced children's class in which Sigung incorporated Kung Fu techniques into forms (katas) and choreographed dance. I did love that class! A few years later

Sigung created a wonderful class on Saturday mornings for adults only. Here he taught the internal martial arts of Chi Gong and Bagua, meditation, spiritual philosophy (which was my first introduction to Buddhist thought), and bits and pieces of Reiki; he also taught that Chi Gong is the foundation of Reiki. While attending this class, I found out that Sigung had initiated many of the other students into Reiki Level II so that students could take care of each other when injured.

Sigung initiated only five or six Reiki masters, and I am blessed to be one of them. I asked him one day if he would give me the initiation--he didn't answer but gave me a meditation exercise to do. Almost three months later, as I was leaving class exhausted and sweaty, Sigung called me into his office and asked me to sit in the chair he had placed in the center of the room. He then gave my Master initiation.

I didn't feel ready to teach, but students were appearing. Sigung taught the old-school way; all teaching was oral and not in an organized way. To make my first Reiki I course manual I combed through 3 years of Chi Gong class notes to pull out the gems of wisdom. With Sigung's support I began teaching at the Xen school, and later opened my own Desert Lotus space. Lao Xie visited El Paso a few times, teaching clinics in martial arts at Xen and therapy at Desert Lotus.

After Sigung's death in 2008, Simo gave me the title of Sifu, or teacher (which Sigung had been planning), and gave her blessing for me to continue teaching the Reiki I learned from Sigung.

Clerical Lineage

MahaVajra

Enlightened spiritual master MahaVajra is my current master and MahAcharya (Grand Bishop) of the Mahajrya Buddhist Tradition. This lineage is infused with the consciousness of Maha's masters—Jesus, Krishna, Melchizedek, and Shakyamuni Buddha.

Maha received initiation and wisdom transmission directly from Usui Sensei through soul level communion. In June of 2009 Maha guided me through this initiation as well.

The dictionary definition of the Sanskrit name MahaVajra is Big Diamond, or Big Lightning Bolt; on a deeper level, it means great strike of enlightenment. Maha is French Canadian, beloved by thousands of world-wide devoted students and disciples. I brought the spiritual techniques included in this book from teachings I personally received from him at many of his US and international seminars. You can find more information about Maha and his teachings at www.mahavajra.com, and also view many seminar recordings on his YouTube channel by searching for "Maha Vajra".

The Importance of Lineage

Each lifetime, our karma brings experiences required for evolution to each of us. We meet who we are supposed to meet, and experience what we are supposed to experience. Our masters are created to be our masters, as we are created to be masters for our students. In this respect, every lineage is perfect for its members.

When a student receives a Reiki initiation, he or she will receive from the Master Teacher the consciousness of Usui Sensei and the Reiki symbols in their body. The consciousness of Usui Sensei itself flows through every student in every lineage. However, this consciousness is flavored with the consciousness of each member of the lineage. Both the distance one is from Usui Sensei on a lineage chart and the level of consciousness of the members of the lineage have an effect on the purity of the consciousness received through initiation. You as an upcoming Mahaananda Master will be only six people away from Usui Sensei through the martial arts lineage and only three people away from Usui Sensei through the clerical lineage. Also, all members of the Mahaananda Reiki lineage are highly spiritual, honorable masters. And this is very auspicious.

The Initiation Experience

The initiation process appears to be similar to a Reiki chair treatment (see the section on Evaluation and Treatment), with the Master Teacher placing his or her hands on or above the chakras of the student. The Master Teacher will also draw symbols on or near the student.

What does it feel like to receive initiation? The feedback from my students is the same as what you can find in just about any book. The physical experiences are vibration or warmth especially in the hands, a feeling of energy flowing and swirling in and around the body, clearer senses, relaxation and calmness, crying, feeling hands other than mine, and seeing colors. One master student felt so much energy flowing for two days that she was unable to sleep. Spiritual experiences include bliss, a feeling of deepened spiritual awareness and intuitive wisdom, a sense of "coming home", and awareness of non-human presences (divine and deceased family members). One experience students have told me about that I haven't seen in other Reiki books is a tendency to have more vivid dreams after the initiation. Occasionally students will see light flowing from my hands, and my aura. Some of these experiences can last for several days. The common teaching is that the Level I initiation is a powerful cleansing process which lasts up to 21 days; that this process could cause headache, vomiting, diarrhea, minor illness, and crying. Sigung simply said, "You'll be cranky for a few days". However, students that are already doing any kind of serious spiritual practice prior to their initiation don't have too much of the cleansing experience.

My experience when receiving my own master initiation from Sigung was that my bones felt like jelly for about seven hours; I could barely drive home that night, or walk around the house. For three days, my awareness was pulled inside myself so strongly that the world around me seemed like a TV in another room—I was aware of it in the background but it really wasn't clear. At the time, I had given my notice at my job and had only three days left. I was so distracted that I really think I might have lost that job, or at least been required to undergo drug testing if I wasn't already on my way out. When Maha introduced me to the consciousness of Usui Sensei, I fell into a state of bliss so joyful that I began to cry and laugh out loud. This experience is still strong, and I am very affected each time I share this process with my own students. When I give initiations, I always feel and faintly see Usui Sensei, Sigung, Lao Xie and Maha in attendance—what a happy honor!

The Transformation from Initiation

Because of the transmission of consciousness, each initiation is a spiritual transformation. But there are also two immediate and obvious physical effects. First, the body (and especially the hands) becomes more sensitive to the physical feel of the resonance of energy. Most of my students are already sensitive to energy prior to initiation, but afterwards the sensations are either more intense or more apparent. This is useful for the therapist's **evaluation** of the flow of energy and whether there is a blockage or imbalance. Next, the body of the student becomes a powerful conduit of energy, which influences the **treatment, or therapy** (powerful in the sense of allowing his or her consciousness to affect another).

Distance Initiation

I used to believe that initiations, because of their sacred nature, should only be done in person. I had some really negative reactions to website and social media on-line initiation advertisements. But I began using Skype as a means of receiving spiritual lessons, and eventually received mantra initiations from Maha and others—and they were quite powerful. So I contemplated the question of why quality distant Reiki *initiations* couldn't be possible when quality distant Reiki *treatments* ARE possible. I didn't find a reason why, and began to give Reiki initiations through Skype while paying close attention to the sacred state of being. My students from all over the world have the same intensity of experiences as my local students.

Playing with Energy

It's good to practice feeling energy after initiation. We have all felt the flow of chi, or energy, in the form of our body's involuntary response to things like fever (chills), or to a first kiss (mmmmm). Now we will practice feeling it **on purpose**. Just like anything else, the more we practice, the better we get.

The following exercise works with the palms of the hands (Lao Gong). As in the left image below, hold your hands loosely in front of you, palm facing palm with fingers gently curved, as if you were holding a cantaloupe. Listen (or open your awareness) for a slight tingling in the palms or fingers. Now, move your hands slowly in a 2-3 inch in-and-out movement—this causes energy to accumulate between them. Listen for a magnetic feeling. When moving out, something seems to be pulling them back in; when moving in, the palms feel as if they are repelling each other. This is quite subtle, but you will become more aware with practice. If you have difficulty, try clapping your hands and rubbing them together briskly before doing the exercise—it can stimulate the energy flow. You might have seen this clapping and rubbing done by Mr. Miyagi before "fixing" Daniel-san in the original Karate Kid movie.

For the next exercise reference the photo on the right. Put your right hand in the Sword Charm mudra by extending your index and middle fingers and anchoring your ring and pinky fingers with your thumb (like a Peace sign but with the extended fingers together). Point the right-hand mudra at your left palm, two to three inches away, making slow spiraling motions with the fingers. Listen for heat or tingling in the left palm. Some students experience a "cool breeze" feeling. Now change hands (left-hand Sword Mudra points at the right hand) and do it again. The purpose of this activity is to see which of your hands is the most sensitive to the feel of energy. Most students have more sensation receiving energy in the left (receiving) hand than in the right (giving) hand. Once you know which hand is the most sensitive, you can take it into consideration when evaluating whether or not two chakras are balanced.

Evaluation and Treatment

Simultaneous Evaluation and Treatment

Treatment consists very simply of placing your hands at the chakras, either directly on the body to make light contact, or a little above it where you can feel a cushion of energy. Here you evaluate the intensity and consistency of the energy, waiting for the feeling to become a gentle heat or tingling. The treatment is complete when the energy of all chakras is consistent and gentle. Or even simpler, placing hands where it hurts, such as on a joint with arthritic pain, or on the lungs to soothe grief. Simpler still, hold someone's hand, or give them a hug. This is effective since energy flows where it is needed; though it's not as efficient as using the major energy gates.

What You as a Therapist Might Experience

The most common sensations that you might experience during a treatment are warmth, vibration, or pressure; less common are cold, waves of energy, a breeze, colors, emotion, or thoughts. The warmth is more intense than just the ambient warmth of your hand next to the body of your client. The vibration feels different to everyone. To me it feels as if I put my hand on the kitchen countertop next to a running food processor, kind of a buzzing feeling. Some students say it feels like tingling, and others say it feels like a mild electric shock—tingling mixed with a slightly numb sensation. Intensity and consistency can be different at various chakras. You might not feel anything at all or almost nothing—this means the chakra is blocked or drawing very little energy. You might feel very intense energy. You might feel an almost solid buzz, or a very prickly sensation. You really don't have to know what the interpretation means, you just need to leave your hands at the chakra until you feel that gentle, consistent energy that indicates balance.

Giving Reiki treatments to pregnant women is a wonderful experience. When you place your hands over the womb you will feel the consistency of the baby's energy very different from that of the mother—you can feel the miracle of life happening under your hands. The baby's energy is so pure and fine; it's like silk compared to the mother's cotton energy. (See the section on Prudence with Certain Treatments.)

If you are very sensitive to energy, you will feel these sensations not just in your hands, but in many parts of your body, especially flowing up through the feet. At times, I feel a "hot flash" through my body associated with one chakra, but not others. I've also felt as if my body became very tall. One of my students never felt a single vibration, but saw colors as her way of evaluating. Two others felt cold rather than heat. If you begin to feel the pain and discomfort of your client—this is because you are an empath, not because you are practicing Reiki.

After a treatment, clients tend to ask "Don't you get tired giving energy all day?" I get tired from standing for a long time and holding my arms out over my clients, but not from the energy flow. Remember that you are merely a conduit; you are not using or giving your own energy. In fact, you are actually getting a bit of a Reiki treatment as the energy flows through your body. I used to get a sinus infection two or three times a year, but since mid-2006 when I began to do a lot of Reiki therapy, I've had only two. I attribute this to the benefit I receive from giving frequent treatments.

What Your Client Might Experience

When receiving a Reiki treatment (or during a self-treatment), a person can receive both benefits (positive changes in physical or emotional states) and experiences (fun). What I share here is not from books, but from people I've treated.

The Benefits

As I mentioned in the introduction section, the most basic benefit of Reiki is stress reduction, which naturally results in many more mental and emotional benefits. Mild depression turns toward happiness, resistance turns toward acceptance, anxiety turns toward peace, anger turns toward compassion, fear turns toward faith, and grief turns toward fond memories. I sometimes speak to clients about karma and dharma, non-attachment and emotional integration—If they want to resolve the cause of their emotional and physical dis-ease (meaning not in a natural harmonious state) as well as the effects of it.

Stress reduction naturally results in physical benefits also. Headaches and migraines disappear; an impending migraine never manifests; anxiety or asthma attacks decrease in frequency, duration and intensity; back and TMJ (jaw) pain decreases or disappears; menstrual pain disappears; numbness decreases; sinuses open up; acid reflux turns sweet; and energy levels rise. Recovery accelerates—recovery from surgery occurs in half the time with half the pain expected by doctors, and a stomach virus that usually lasts four days lasts for only two. Because the entire illness is compressed into less time, the experience will probably be intense. Sigung once got a hematoma about the size of an egg as a result of sparring during martial arts class. One of the students who knew Reiki put his hands over it for 15 minutes and it disappeared. Most people that have trouble falling or staying asleep report the best night's sleep they can remember on the day they had a Reiki treatment.

Every now and then a benefit appears in disguise, with discomfort or even pain. Rarely, a client will develop pain during a treatment that wasn't there before the treatment. This is an energy blockage being forcibly opened by a strong energy flow, and the pain is gone by the end of the treatment. One of my clients experienced heart palpitations during her first treatment, which was very frightening for her as she had been diagnosed with heart problems. She had no intention of ever returning for additional Reiki, but at her next cardiologist visit she was informed that her heart condition had improved. Prior to this visit, she had been told that her condition was a type that would never improve, and would only get worse. She became a regular client and also a Reiki student.

Benefits range from nothing noticeable (this is rare) to what might be called miraculous (also rare). Why? Some say that Reiki requires belief, or a kind of mental cooperation to achieve benefits. I agree with this to some extent. However, when I worked at the R&R Center, Reiki treatments were not optional. At the beginning of their first Reiki treatment some very blunt young soldiers were happy to tell me that they did not believe in "this b***s***" and were only in my treatment room because they didn't have a choice. I would smile, gently say "that's OK", and proceed. Only two of these doubting soldiers left at the end of their first treatment with the same opinion ☺. The most important thing that governs the effectiveness of a Reiki treatment is karma. If it is one's karma (or according to the path God planned for you) to become well, Reiki will help do this. If perfect health is not your karma, Reiki will not be a miracle cure.

<u>The Fun</u>

Now for the "fun". Your client might experience the energy flow similar to the way you could, in the form of warmth, vibration, pressure, light, emotion, or thought. I've been asked several times if I use a heating pad during treatments. It's common for a client to feel energy flowing through their body, swirling around, especially in the head, or popping up somewhere other than where the Reiki-ist's hands are positioned. The body takes the energy where it is needed. Also common for the client is phantom hands—still feeling your hands at an area after you have moved on to another area, or feeling that there are several pairs of hands on their body. My understanding of this is that the chakra(s) is now open and flowing more strongly even after you are no longer there.

The client might feel a light or floating sensation, or a dense heavy sinking sensation, in their body which are results of a deep meditative state created by the Reiki. Several of my clients have experienced differences in the right and left side of the body—feeling that one side was higher than the other; either in a stair step way, or that the body was slanted. One side of the body might be perceived as being a different color than the other side of the body. I once had a client, who after his treatment began inspecting the underside of the Reiki table, looking for cables. He had a rather intense sensation that the table itself had been moving, the head and foot of it being raised and lowered. Another, while my hands were on his feet, felt as if his body raised up into an almost standing position, with only his feet still touching the table.

The client can be awake, but also asleep at some level—experiencing a dream they are having, or vivid memories whose details reside only in the depths of the subconscious mind. It's common for a client to be snoring, and at the same time to be aware that they are snoring. One client actually thought that her Reiki therapist (a good friend of mine) had fallen asleep during the treatment because she heard snoring, not even considering that it was she herself doing the snoring. Some people feel the presence of others in the room, or even assisting with the therapy (sometimes along with the phantom hands). Another client spontaneously laughed out loud with joy for several minutes when my hands were on his Crown chakra—he said the feeling reminded him of the joy and freedom of childhood play.

I've described a lot of possible types of "fun", but most clients will experience only a few of these during a treatment. Maybe two of every ten will experience a variety of sensations. And, there is the rare person that doesn't experience anything other than a feeling of peace. This doesn't mean that the treatment wasn't beneficial; it means only that the person was not aware of the "fun". Say that there are two people—the first has a great sense of smell, and the second doesn't smell much of anything. If the first one smells a rose, the diaphragm moves down, drawing air in over the flower petals (along with tiny particles of the petals) into the lungs. The rose particles stimulate sensors in the nose, and the information travels to the brain. Ah, it smells so wonderful! If the second one smells a rose, the diaphragm moves down, drawing air in over the flower petals into the lungs. The rose particles stimulate sensors in the nose, and the information did not travel to the brain, or the brain did not recognize it—all the same things happened, but there is no conscious awareness of "fun". Those in this situation (including myself before I began my spiritual path), will develop much more awareness of the feel of energy or consciousness along with more meditation and exposure to energy treatment.

Hand Positions and Treatment

How to Hold Your Hands

From my own experience, there is no right or wrong way to hold your hands. But some beginners (like me when I was beginning) are concerned that if they use incorrect hand positions it will diminish the effectiveness of their treatment, so the traditional way is as follows:

- Fingers and thumbs are together with no spaces between
- Hold your hands side by side, with thumbs and tips of index fingers touching (for a compact, round surface area) OR
- Hold your hands end to end, with the tips of the index and middle finger of one hand touching the base of the thumb on the other hand (for an elongated surface area)
- Beaming—stand away from your client and point the palm of your right hand toward her, with your left palm extended toward Heaven (this is a "shotgun" approach for treatment which addresses the entire energetic system in a less intense way).

Sometimes I keep my hands touching when working with one chakra at a time. Other times I work with two chakras at a time, and other times I have my hands at the front and back of one chakra. Still other times I might reach my left hand to Heaven, with my right hand on a chakra. I just do what feels right at the time. One point to keep in mind if you will not be using both hands at the same chakra is that the left hand is the receiving hand, and the right hand is the giving hand—so when using only one hand, use the right hand if it's possible.

Hands On or Hands Off

When I first began accepting payment for Reiki therapy, I was concerned about legal issues. Some states require a license to practice Reiki—it falls under the category of "body work" and the Reiki-ist must obtain a massage therapy license. This is not yet the case in Texas, although it has been addressed in the state legislature several times. Reiki is not body work, it is energy work—there is no physical manipulation of muscle or other tissue. (Please research and follow the laws in your state.) Still, I wanted to be careful about the appearance of practicing massage without a license, so my hand position was always "hands off". This question was raised at a therapy class taught by Lao Xie in November of 2007. His guidance was that touch itself is therapeutic, so we should always touch when we can. And so I began to use the hands-on position.

With practice, I discovered that my sensitivity to the feel of energy is stronger with the hands-off position. So, now I use a combination of hands off for evaluation, and hands on for treatment. About 80% of my students find this to be true for themselves also. For the most part though, it doesn't seem to make a difference to the client.

- Hands on—softly rest your hands on your client, or on yourself during a self-treatment. There should only be enough pressure to make a light contact.
- Hands off—hands are a few inches above the body. Find where you feel the most sensation of energy, it feels rather like a cushion of air. I call this the "sweet spot".

Of course, to be considerate of your client and to avoid any legal difficulties, never touch personal areas. Always use hands-off for the Base chakra. For male clients, use hands off for the Sacral chakra; and for female clients, use hands off for the Heart chakra. There is the rare person who never likes to be touched, even won't have a gentle Swedish massage—so be sure to ask about this before their treatment. Also take care of yourself. If you are very sensitive to the energies of others, it's fine to use the hands-off position.

Where to Place Your Hands

What will you try to accomplish? How much time do you have? What are the social circumstances? All these questions and more will help you decide what hand positions you want to use. Most important, if you have intuition, trust yourself and use it.

Whatever hand positions you use, you simply leave your hands at each chakra until you feel a gentle sensation, which is consistent between chakras when you're working with more than one. Sometimes a student new to energy work or spiritual practices might not feel much energy while doing a treatment, or might not be drawn by intuition to particular chakras. In this is your case, you can use one of the basic roadmaps outlined below.

And then there's the "Quick Fix". Just put your hands where it hurts—maybe a headache, anxiety felt in the stomach, or a sprained ankle—until it feels better. We all know that many times the cause of an ailment is not where the ailment manifests. A headache might be caused by stress, low blood sugar, high blood pressure, allergies, strained eyes, paint fumes, or many other things. If we don't have the time to treat the entire body, just treat the effect. It still helps, even if it might not fix the whole problem.

You can't do Reiki "wrong"; you're only assisting the body to do what it does naturally. What if in your treatment you didn't work with *all* of the chakras, you had to stop working on a chakra before it felt balanced, or you think you might have treated the wrong chakra? Don't worry—remember that the Sushumna (Central Channel) connects all of the major chakras from Base to Crown, so working with any one chakra affects all other chakras to some extent. The body moves the energy to where it's needed. Even our physical body draws energy where it's needed, and it does this naturally at the cellular level to heal itself. Imagine you are preparing a meal, and cut your finger, and it later becomes infected. Every cell in the body knows about it. Extra white blood cells are created throughout the body and receive information from the Nadi system, all flowing through the blood to exactly where they are needed—to the infection in your finger. Here they devour the bacterial cells. Why wouldn't this happen on an energetic level also? Working directly with the chakras which are blocked or resonating more or less intensely than the others is not the only way to do a productive therapy session—it is simply more efficient.

Being Careful with Certain Treatments

There are some circumstances in which you should limit the amount of therapy you provide. I'm noting a few of them here which Sigung taught as examples—but use your intuition.

- Broken Bones: Using Reiki on a possible broken bone before it is set properly could actually slow down the reconstruction process. The bone fragments will begin to regenerate, rounding off the edges of the splintered bone, and the "pieces of the puzzle" will not fit as perfectly together when set. This results in more space between the bone fragments, requiring more bone growth.

- Children and Pets: Children and small pets are very sensitive to Reiki—it's best to limit the duration of each treatment to 30 minutes or less. Pets will let you know; they will walk away when they are done with you. Parents of a newborn baby who was scheduled for heart surgery asked me to do some distant Reiki (see Level II Reiki) for their child. After meditating on the best way to do the treatments, I ended up somewhat following a newborn's typical eating pattern—I did about 10 minutes every 2 to 3 hours. If you are working on a pregnant woman, it's normal for the baby to begin moving and kicking a lot, so this tells you when your treatment is over.

- Mental Illness: Reiki is not generally suggested for treating serious mental illness which expresses itself as difficulty distinguishing between reality and illusion. Experiencing the "fun" of a Reiki treatment could be very disturbing to this kind of client.

Self-Treatment

For self-treatment, you can work only with the major chakras, or you can also add placing your hands at each of the major joints and soles of the feet. Just do what your body tells you to do. I like to Reiki the major chakras in the morning when I'm taking a shower. I see more colors here, and the vibration of the water as it hits my body adds a little to the experience. I've also used Reiki at night to help me fall asleep. Here are the hand positions with suggested order.

1 - Crown

2 - 3rd Eye

3 - Pineal Gland (hands at ears)

4 - Jade Gate

5 - Throat

6 - Heart

7 - Solar Plexus

8 - Sacral

9 – Base

Treating Others

Give a Little Love

Place your right hand on your friend or client's shoulder or at the Host Chakra (Yang Diamond) during a greeting or conversation.

The Chair Treatment

One of my master students was an elementary school teacher, and every day when she entered the Teachers' Lounge a line had already formed to receive her popular free chair treatments. This treatment addresses the eight major chakras plus the pineal gland, and is very useful in a work, health fair or seminar setting—or any time you have just a few minutes. Start at the top and move down, finishing with the entire Central channel. Suggested hand position and order are shown below.

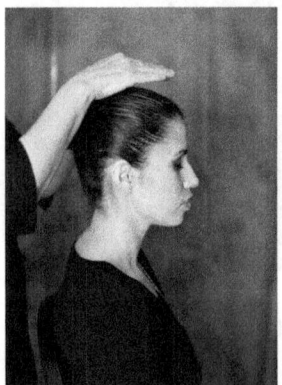

1 - Crown

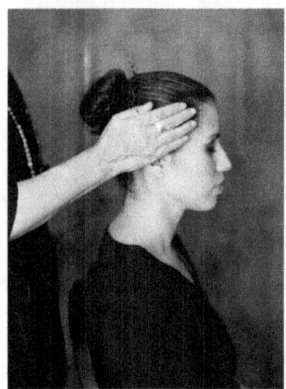

2 - Pineal (hands at ears)

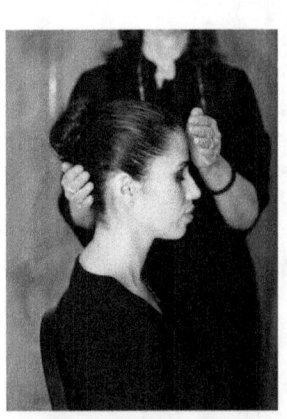

3 - 3rd Eye/Jade Gate

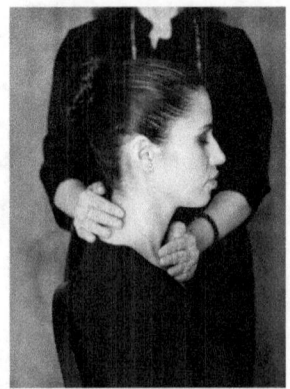

4 - Throat

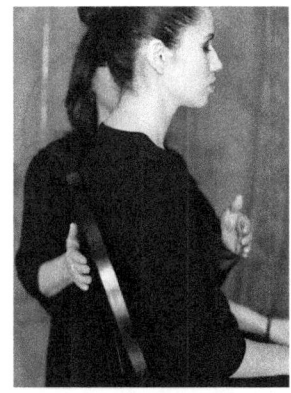
5 - Heart

6 - Solar Plexus

7 - Sacral

8 - Base

9 - Crown/Base

The Table Treatment

You'll be performing a more formal and comprehensive type of treatment on a table. I use a Reiki table, which is a customized massage table—at the head and foot of the table the x-shaped leg supports of a typical massage table are replaced with an arch, so that the Reiki practitioner can sit comfortably by scooting in with her legs under the table. I recommend adjusting the table height to your own hip level so that you can lean against the table when your hand positions require you to stand. This minimizes the stress on your back caused by standing and holding your arms out and over your client during the treatment. And try to set up the table in a way that allows you to mover around it easily.

Preparing for a table treatment:

- Given the circumstances, create as pleasant and conducive an environment as possible. Quiet any noise, turn down the lights, and put on some relaxing music or water sounds. Silence your cell phone and request your client to do so also. I don't usually light scented candles or incense because it bothers a lot of people, but I do have them ready if a client requests it.
- For a first-time client, briefly explain what they can expect during the treatment—what you will be doing and what "fun" they might experience.
- Ask your client about any physical limitations and accommodate them; such as difficulty lying on their back for a long time, or acid reflux issues while lying flat. I learned the hard way that if you don't ask, they probably won't tell you. One of my first clients was in a lot of pain after her treatment—and it was pain she didn't have before the treatment. She knew that lying on her back would hurt her, but didn't think to ask if she could turn on her side because she assumed that it was necessary to be on her back for Reiki to work. If your client suffers from acid reflux you can prop her up with pillows under the upper back and head.
- Have your client remove their glasses and shoes.
- Wash your hands. Besides being good hygiene, it's a ritual of purification and preparation.

The traditional approach to performing general balancing treatment is simple—start from the top with either the 3rd Eye or Crown chakra, and then work your way down (see the sequence of hand positions below). Leave your hands at each chakra until you feel a gentle sensation. If you don't feel the energy, just stay at each chakra for five minutes—it's still going to work. This procedure is a kind of road map for new therapists, therapists that don't feel much energy, or therapists that aren't intuitive. That was me when I first began my Reiki work, but constant practice at awareness while doing therapy over the years has made me very sensitive to the feel of energy. Even now environmental conditions can prevent me from feeling much energy; such as when it is very cold in the therapy room or when there is air blowing over my hands.

If you are intuitive, first treat where you are drawn to treat. Messages come in many ways, such as thinking about a certain chakra, feeling energy in your own body, or feeling an emotion. Then, continue to perform general balancing of the entire body. In my experience, practicing transmigration and emotional integration is a wonderful way to develop intuition. If your client doesn't mind helping you learn, ask for feedback when you think you have received some intuitive information.

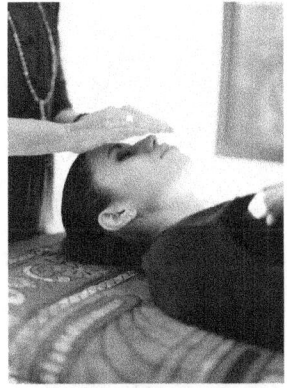

1 - 3rd Eye

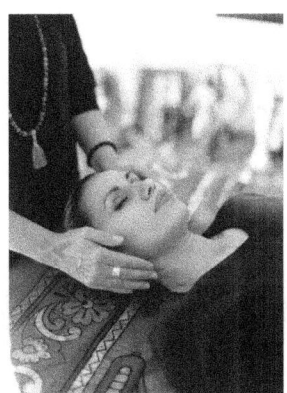

2 - Pineal Gland

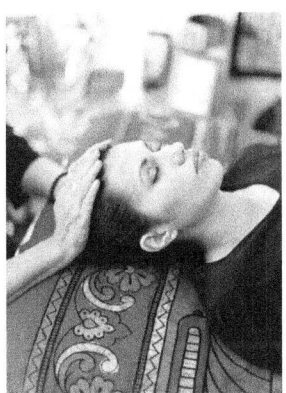

3 - Crown

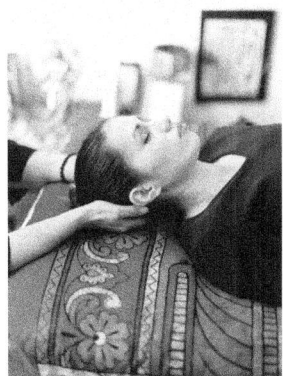

4 - Jade Gate

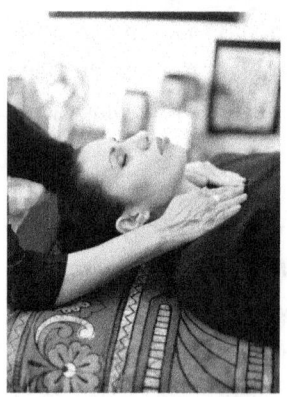
5 - Throat

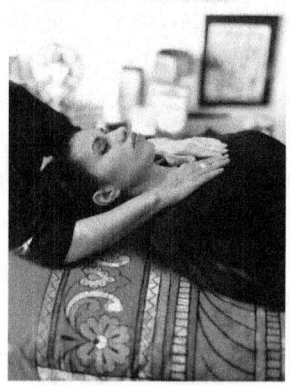
6 - Top of Lungs

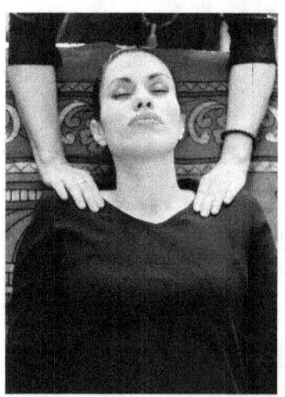
7 - Shoulders

8 - Heart

9 - Solar Plexus

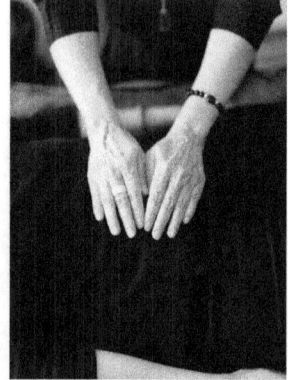
10 – Dan-Tian

11 – Sacral

12 - Base

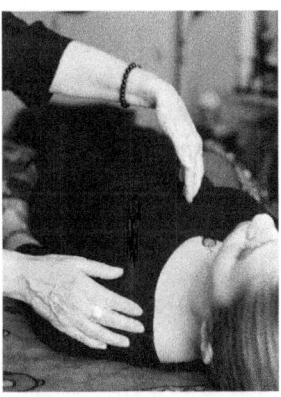

13 - Heart/Shoulder

14 - Shoulder/Elbow

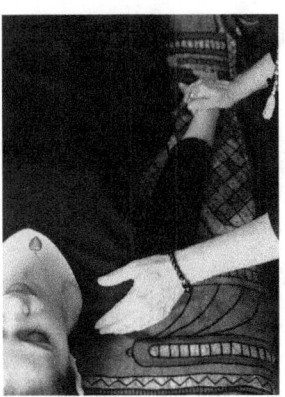

15 - Shoulder/Wrist

16 - Hips

17 - Hip/Knee

18 - Ankles

19 - Ankle/Yong Quan

20 – Yong Quan (both)

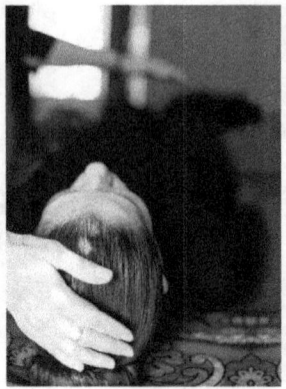
21 - Crown/Base

After the treatment,

- Conclude the session by "brushing" the aura. Use both of your hands in a sweeping motion from 3rd Eye to the feet (a few inches above the body), then into the earth. This is an optional step which I personally don't usually perform, but some therapists really like it.
- Gently rouse your client and offer her some water.
- Share what you both experienced.
- After your client leaves you can brush your own aura—this is like brushing dust off of your clothing from shoulders to ankles.
- After each treatment, purify yourself by washing your hands with cool water and meditating (see the section below on Suggestions for Evaluation and Treatment).

Group Therapy

You may participate with several other Reiki-ists to provide a group treatment for a client; each of you concentrating on one or several hand positions. This is a wonderful way to give an intense, short treatment. After observing and participating in this type of treatment in social settings, I recommend that at least one of the therapists follow up with a full body scan following the treatment in order to confirm that all chakras are balanced. Also, be mindful that this kind of treatment can be overwhelming to an empathic client.

Sigung once allowed me to invite a dear friend of mine to the Xen Academy. She had been in a very bad car accident and was temporarily confined to a wheel chair while multiple severe injuries were healing. Six students from the Chi Gong class did a group Reiki treatment for her—she said it felt like being in the ocean, being lifted and lowered by large swells of water. She found it very pleasant, but also had trouble sleeping for a few days because of the energy still flowing through her body.

How to Use Spiritual Techniques for Yourself When Doing Therapy

Preparation—Moving into the Sacred State of Being
- Wash your hands for good hygiene, and also as symbolic of purification.
- Acknowledge the gift and guidance of Usui Sensei, Sigung and Maha—feel their consciousness.
- Practice self-awareness—of your body, energy, emotions and thoughts.
- Consciously raise the power (for personal preparation and protection) of the Elements, Peace, Compassion and Three Suns by doing a few recitations of each mantra.
- Open yourself to service with love. Release any expectations or attachment to the outcome of your treatment. Attaching to the outcome involves your ego, and could also influence your client's process of working through their own karma. "God, may Thy will be done".

Treatment
- Use your preferred hand positions, either touching the body, or just at the level where you feel the energy, usually two to three inches above the body.
- Remember that it is not you doing or directing the therapy; you are only a conduit of energy, and the body takes the energy where it is needed.
- Simply wait to feel the change. You are looking for gentle warmth or vibration (or however you experience energy), the same intensity at all the chakras.

Closing and Rejuvenation
- Express gratitude for the opportunity to make Reiki therapy available to your client (or to yourself). Bow to your client.
- After each treatment, purify yourself by washing your hands with cool water and meditating a short while.
- Replenish in yourself the power of the Elements, Peace, Compassion and Three Suns by doing a few recitations of each mantra.

The Five Precepts

Usui Sensei's Reiki teachings include "The Five Precepts", which expand Reiki into a lifestyle. He taught that these affirmations should be spoken each morning and each evening. The emperor of Japan had given these Precepts as a gift to the Japanese people during the very stressful days of the arrival (or invasion) of Western trade and culture, and Usui Sensei subsequently drew this wisdom of present moment and compassion into Reiki. Here is the wording as taught by Lao Xie:

1. As I live in this Moment, I will release my anger, frustration, resentment and grief... it is already past

2. As I live in this Moment, I will release my fear and worry... nothing has happened yet, though I can choose to create it negatively or positively

3. As I live in this Moment, I will have gratitude for all that I have in my life

4. As I live in this Moment, I will honor my ancestors and myself by conducting myself honestly

5. As I live in this Moment, I will have respect for all others and treat them as I would like to be treated

Follow the Middle Way in Mind, Body & Spirit

Mahaananda Reiki Level II

Level II Spiritual Techniques

The First Two Siddhis

Siddhis are contemplative meditations on a single word which expand your perception. The Sanskrit word "siddhi" (pronounced "*sih*-dee"), which translates to power or accomplishment, refers to supernatural powers that can be attained by the practice of yoga. The meaning of yoga here is the original one—a spiritual discipline that leads to a state of union with God. You can study all of the siddhis in "The Yoga Sutras of Patanjali".

Do this meditation on each siddhi for approximately 20 minutes per day, for a period of 33 days—and the 33 days don't have to be consecutive. Finish your 33 days on the first siddhi before meditating on the second siddhi. *(Don't say the mantra word aloud except when teaching or meditating—in conversation you might refer to the first siddhi, or the smallest siddhi).*

The effect of siddhi meditation is like placing a tea bag in hot water—the feeling of it will softly permeate throughout you. Begin each of the siddhi meditations by breathing, paying attention inside, calming the mind, and observing that you are aware of yourself. Softly and slowly repeat the mantra to yourself, eventually thinking it silently, while contemplating the meaning. After a few minutes, let go of the philosophical contemplation and remain in a state of awareness while you repeat the mantra. Just be available for discovery without asking a question—a question is too active. Come back to the mental contemplation only if you notice that your mind is wandering, and then let it go again.

First Siddhi

Philosophy

The mantra is "anima", pronounced "*ah*-nee-mah". Anima means the smallest, most subtle, softest level of the universe. Your goal in the first siddhi is for your perception to come from so small a point of view that you can perceive nothing but waves of energy, or vibration. It is to become aware of existence at the level of the space between atoms, at the level of the universal substance, which makes up everything and is between everything. Practicing this siddhi will help you let go of your sense of individual definition (your identity) for a while, so you can unattach from it.

Meditation

Close your eyes, go inside yourself, and breathe. Be aware that you are aware. Relax your body; begin to relax the point of view of your perception. Pay attention to your body. What does it feel like from the inside? Begin by paying attention to your skin, then your muscles, then your organ systems, then your liver (chemical reactions), then the liver cells, then the atoms, and then the space between the atoms. Smaller and smaller, sinking in between particles, losing density. Finally, your perception is so subtle that nothing is defined anymore. Let yourself disappear. Your consciousness is absorbed in the most minute, subtle, soft, still substance at the base of all things. You are contemplating supreme consciousness, the fabric of the universe.

I entered this in my meditation journal when I first began meditating on the first siddhi: "It is the most delicate of vibrations. The grosser vibrations of the physical, emotional and mental consciousness are no longer perceptible. My sense of identity, of self, dissolves. I am like a drop of water, but not a drop, in the depths of the deepest sea, where no wave can disturb me. All I am aware of is this delicate vibration, everywhere. I can hear the vibration, the almost imperceptible hum; it is the sound of Om".

Second Siddhi

Philosophy

The mantra is "mahima", pronounced "*mah*-hee-mah". It means all-pervading, most immense, biggest, greatest consciousness. Your goal is to expand your perception into the immensity of all creation—it's the universal view of the anima vibration—you are aware of this vibration as it manifests even at the level of galaxies through the dancing of the five elements. With the first siddhi, you come to a point of perception so small and subtle that immensity naturally reveals itself and you fall into the consciousness of the second siddhi.

Meditation

Close your eyes, go inside yourself, and breathe. Be aware that you are aware. Pay attention to your physical body, and then to your body as manifested consciousness. Gradually expand your perception beyond your body—into the room you are sitting in, into the building you are in, into the neighborhood, into the city, into the planet, into the universe—let go of the limits of your consciousness. Expand into the universal substance, which is made of the *potential for all of creation* (the Five Elements). Become aware of the elements, all flowing together. Feel the Earth, the stars, and the galaxies. It's not that you are growing larger; you are simply becoming conscious that you and your awareness already exist throughout the entire universe. Lose yourself in the immensity. Observe everything in the universe from the point of view of the universe. The flow of consciousness in a tiny flower is the same as the flow in an enormous star.

My journal entry for the second siddhi was "I am not a drop of water in the ocean. I am the ocean; the drop of water is inside me. The universe resides in me."

Transmigration

Transmigration is a technique you use to taste and influence the state of being of someone else; in other words, to evaluate and treat your client. To transmigrate is to expand the awareness of your own consciousness to also include your "target"—you become conscious of the other's state of being, and then affect it. Because your Soul exists everywhere, not just in your body, you can choose to be aware outside of your body. Your meditation on the first two siddhis will help you achieve this expanded perception.

Find a partner who is open to these concepts to join you in this practice; each partner will take a turn doing the active practice and then receiving. Do your best to be attentive and relaxed in order to feel the effects of the activities described here, because they can be quite subtle. Remember that you already do this—you are now fine-tuning your awareness so that it is conscious. Share your experience with your partner and help each other.

Influencing Chi

Here are six simple exercises which demonstrate that your perception, or soul, does extend outside of you and that you can affect things outside of your own body. Energy, or chi, is tangible consciousness, and we can affect it simply by paying attention.

- First exercise: (*This is the same exercise you did in Reiki Level I to practice feeling energy.*) This can be done with your own hand, or the hand of a partner. With your right hand, point with either one or two fingers to the palm of your own left hand from several inches away. Place your attention on the left palm, and forcefully shoot energy into it from the right-hand fingers. Feel the effect of heat or vibration in the left hand. You can move your right hand in a spiral or circular movement to see how that feels. Then move the pointing fingers of your right hand slowly down your left arm to the elbow, and back up. Share your experiences with your partner.

- Second exercise: Stand 4-6 feet away from your partner. With your right hand, point with either one or two fingers and forcefully shoot chi into the outstretched left palm of your partner, who focuses on feeling it.

Direct Energy to Own Hand

Direct Energy to Other's Hand

Technique for Transmigration

Next we will move from directing energy to placing attention inside your client. This is how I transmigrate:

- Pay attention inside (become aware of yourself).
- Observe yourself being aware of yourself.
- Gently expand your awareness to include your client—there is no separation, no difference.

When I first began to try this in 2009, I wasn't able to do it—I experimented a lot until I finally succeeded. Here are some other methods used by my spiritual friends—so if at first you can't transmigrate easily, maybe one of these techniques will help you.

- Concentrate on your client until you see yourself as a tiny body inside the body of your client. From there, observe.
- Pay attention to your client until you feel an emotion, and then follow the emotion in.
- Meditate on the first siddhi until you feel you have become very small. Then go inside your client, *become* your client, and pay attention.
- If you can't feel it, imagine it. Then your actual experience will follow.

If it still seems impossible, I recommend that you try emotional integration, focusing on the denials. Maybe there is fear, pride, or shame blocking your experience.

Transmigration Exercises

Transmigration into Water

Take an unopened bottle of water, open it and take a drink. What does it taste like? Do you taste the minerals along the sides and back of your tongue, the sweetness, even the consistency of the water? Feel the energy that emanates into your body from the water as it flows into your stomach. What does it feel like?

- Third exercise: Hold the water bottle in your left hand and place your attention in the water for a few minutes, doing your best to "become" the water. Now taste it again. That subtle difference in taste and feel is the influence your soul had on the water, because you observed it.

- Fourth exercise: Now pay attention to the water and chant one of the mantras that you learned, let's say it's Peace, until you feel it strongly in your body. Take a drink of the water. When you feel the energy emanate through your body, see if it feels something like "Peace".

Transmigration in a Water Bottle

Transmigration into a Person

Sit facing your partner; close enough for knees to almost touch.

- Fifth exercise: Your partner places the back of her left hand on her left knee, presenting the left palm to you. Pay attention inside yourself, breathe and be present. Next, expand your attention to your partner's extended left palm (you are paying attention inside yourself and to your partner's palm). Now, also go inside the hand; *be* the hand. Silently chant a mantra or feel a state of being for about 30 seconds. Partners share their experience with each other—what it felt like when you observed, and then what it felt like when you did the mantra.

- Sixth exercise: Pay attention inside yourself, and also in the torso of your partner—Throat, Heart or Solar Plexus chakra. Go inside the torso. Silently chant a mantra or feel a state of being for about 30 seconds. Partners share their experiences of observation and of mantras with each other.

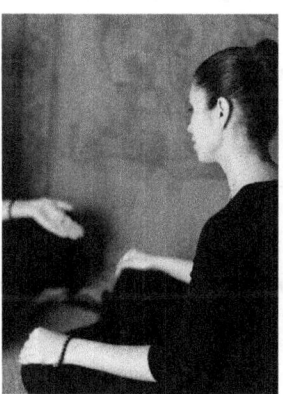

Transmigration in the Hand

Using Transmigration during Therapy

Protect Yourself

Chanting the Earth mantra will help protect you from being affected by the mental and emotional state of those with whom you interact. Even those who seem to be clean and stable might be suffering from mental turmoil or repressed emotions.

If you have already been affected, the Peace and Compassion mantras and Emotional Integration will help bring your mind back to peace and stability, and relieve your heart of some hidden or obvious pain. And integration will also bring you higher sensitivity—when you relieve a mental block or an emotional clog, it becomes much easier to perceive the subtle worlds and even interact with them.

Evaluation (Observation)

- Transmigrate into your client using whatever technique works best for you. At this point, you may become aware of an emotion, depression, or the location of the pain; you may feel and understand that an emotion is the cause of physical pain. Maybe you will just feel the consciousness of your client without interpreting anything. It's okay if you don't feel something—you will still be able to affect your her in a positive way.

Treatment (State of Being)

- Once you are aware of your existence in your client, change your own state of being in order to affect her.
    - Chant mantras (that you have already charged) which are efficient for therapy, such as the minor elemental mantras or the more specific well-being mantras.
    - Or simply sink yourself into a state of being, such as peace or happiness.
- Using these techniques along with Reiki: Reiki just flows because you act as a conduit. When transmigrating and using mantras, you purposely invoke the therapeutic power of a state of being (mantras).

The Peaceful Soul

This mantra brings peace, happiness, and a powerful awareness of the soul in the body. It is very helpful for depression.

"Om mama Om mama Om mama
Atma sukhi bhava sukhi bhava sukhi bhava
Atma shanti shanti shanti
Avaham avaham avaham"

Om	"ohm"	Universal syllable
Mama	"mah-mah"	Divine mother, twice
Atma	"*aht*-mah"	The soul
Sukhi	"*soo*-key"	Happiness
Bhava	"*bah*-vah"	To generate
Shanti	"*shahn*-tee"	Peace
Avaham	"ah-vah-*hahm*"	Make it to exist (Amen)

The peaceful soul mantra invokes the soothing and nurturing consciousness of Divine Mother to care for you and to help your soul generate happiness and peace. Reciting each phrase three times affects the mind, heart and body.

Charging this mantra for yourself: do one mala per day for 41 days.

Charging this mantra to help others: do one mala per day for 108 days. You can do it in less time by doing up to four malas per day, but it is best to not finish the entire process in less than 41 days.

The Well-Being Mantras

Charging the five elemental mantras of Earth, Fire, Heaven, Water and Air brings a higher awareness of the potential for all creation—and along with this a more powerful ability to manifest and transform with therapy. Charging the mantras of Peace, Compassion, and Three Suns brings simple states of being which are the most powerful for spiritual evolution. The well-being mantras will naturally be more powerful for you if you have already charged these elemental and "general" mantras because they create the foundation for the more specific therapeutic properties of the well-being mantras.

Charge these mantras in any order using the formula of 9 malas per day for 12 consecutive days (or one mala per day for 41 consecutive days for the longer mantras—these are noted below).

Most students study these mantras so they can help others—however when charging them, think only of your own body and emotions so that their properties become a part of you. Begin by breathing, paying attention inside, calming the mind, and observing that you are aware of yourself. Contemplate the mantra, focus on whatever needs therapy inside you, and do your japa.

Purification of the Body

This mantra supernaturally purifies your body.

"Om Dhim Hrim Deha Prakshalana"

Om	"ohm"	Universal syllable
Dhim	"deem"	Physical substance
Hrim	"hreem"	Purification
Deha	"*day*-hah"	Body or envelope
Prakshalana	"prahk-shah-*lah*-nah"	Cleanse or purify

Visualize Divine mother pouring cleansing water on and through your body. There is golden radiance in the water and in your body. Dhim is the concept of the Divine incarnated in your body, so Dhim Hrim means Divine purification. It transforms your body to its original pure state. Deha prakshalana expresses again the cleansing of the body. You can use this mantra for treating viral or bacterial infections, Candida, allergies, or an insect bite or sting, among other things. I've also used it to treat tumors.

Regeneration of the Body

This mantra treats physical damage in your body.

"Om Dhim Ra Ra Deha Siddhyaroga"

Om	"ohm"	Universal syllable
Dhim	"deem"	Physical substance
Ra Ra	"rah-rah"	Activation
Deha	"*day*-hah"	Body or envelope
Siddhi	"*si*-dee"	Perfection or empowerment
Aroga	"ah-*roh*-gah"	Health

Force your mind to imagine and then *know* that your body is perfectly healthy and empowered from the level of the cells to the entire body, and feel gratitude to Divine Mother. Dhim Ra Ra activates Divine energies in the body. Deha Siddhyaroga means my body is in a state of perfect health. Use this form of the mantra to improve general health.

For a specific ailment, focus on the ailment. Replace "Deha Siddhyaroga" with "(this body part) is perfectly healthy" in your own language. For example, "Om Dhim Ra Ra my ankle is perfectly healthy". Use this mantra for treating a twisted ankle, the heart muscle after a heart attack, a stomach ulcer, etc.

Soothing Emotional Wounds

This mantra brings happiness and peace to your heart.

"Om Klim Ra Ra Hrdaya Sukhi Shanti"

Om	"ohm"	Universal syllable
Klim	"kleem"	Desires and feelings
Ra Ra	"rah-rah"	Activation
Hrdaya	"her-*die*-yah"	Physical or emotional heart
Sukhi	"*soo*-kee"	Happiness
Shanti	"*shahn*-tee"	Peace

Force your mind to imagine and then *know* that your heart is perfectly harmonious and happy, and feel gratitude to Divine Mother. Gently accept the emotions you feel, but focus on the attitude of soothing the heart. Klim is the experience of emotional yearning; Klim Ra Ra invokes divine energies to soothe the suffering of attachments.

Use this mantra to treat a broken heart or depression.

Clearing Negative Thinking

This mantra transforms the negative mind and heart to a positive state of being.

"Om Aïm Klim Hrim Jaya Bodhicitta Mangala"

Om	"ohm"	Universal syllable
Aim	"ah-*eem*"	Wisdom or knowledge
Klim	"kleem"	Desires and feelings
Hrim	"hreem"	Purification
Jaya	"*jie*-yuh"	Victory
Bodhicitta	"boh-dee-*chee*-tah"	Perfected mind and heart
Mangala	"*mahng*-gah-lah"	Favorable or positive

Feel gratitude to Divine Mother for help in keeping your thoughts and emotions pure and positive. During your practice, do your best to not think about the particular thing that is causing your pessimistic thoughts—the most powerful therapy comes from the general attitude that *everything* is always fine, that you see *everything* as positive. You can charge this mantra with either the 9x12 formula, or 1 mala per day for 41 days.

Positive Thinking Mantra

"Om Jaya Bodhicitta"

This mantra means victory of the perfected mind and heart. Use this portion of the Clearing Negative Thinking mantra by itself when you need immediate positive thinking—a quick fix. If you have already charged the mantra for Clearing Negative Thinking, you don't need to charge this one. If you didn't yet charge the mantra for Clearing Negative Thinking, charge this one using the 9 x 12 formula.

Purifying Chemical Dependence

Almost everyone lives with some level of dependence or craving for alcohol, drugs, cigarettes, caffeine, sugar, salt or other substance (I'll refer to this object of our dependence as a "cookie"). The body mourns and yearns for its cookie when it is missing from the bloodstream, and the heart and body mourn the emotional habit of eating the cookie—we express love and care for our self, or even enjoy our identity, when eating the cookie. For example, if you stop taking smoke breaks at work, you could have the feeling that you no longer give yourself permission to take a stress break. Or if you go on a low-carb diet and stop eating tortillas, you might miss the feeling of your Latino heritage. To stop eating the cookie can bring a feeling of being lost and alone. We treat dependence on cookies with a combination of physical purification of the blood and mental self-reliance and self-love. The steps below will guide you to help yourself, but emotional integration is essential for success.

Getting Ready to Stop Eating Your Cookie

Maybe you're not really ready to stop eating your cookie completely, but you want to test the waters to see what it would be like, or you want to start working on quitting one small step at a time. Spend one day without eating your cookie. At the end of the day, put the cookie in front of you, and while looking at it recite one mala of the *Chemical Dependency Purification Mantra* (CDPM) explained below. This will awaken the yearning, allowing you to feel and observe the experience—to integrate it. The next day you can continue eating your cookie again.

Once You Are Ready to Completely Stop Eating Your Cookie

Once you are ready to stop eating your cookie, don't eat it at all for 12 days. During each of these days, recite 9 malas of the CDPM all at one sitting (or do it for 50 minutes to an hour). Every time you have a reaction to the absence of your cookie—physical or emotional—pay attention to it, feel it, and do your emotional integration. If you break the process, either by missing a day of the mantras or by eating your cookie, start the entire process over again from day one.

After the 12 days are over, do one mala of each of the Five Elements and as many malas of the CDPM as you want to every day. Do this until you might think "it would be nice or wonderful to have a cookie", but you can observe it without much suffering. After this point, please do not tempt yourself by keeping cookies around, or by hanging out with others who eat cookies.

Chemical Dependency Purification Mantra (CDPM)

This mantra purifies your body and blood and helps break emotional habits.

"Om Dhim Hrim Krim Deha Raktaamala Swaasthya"

Om	"ohm"	Universal syllable
Dhim	"deem"	Physical substance
Hrim	"hreem"	Purification
Krim	"kreem"	Break habits
Deha	"*day*-ha"	Body or envelope
Raktaamala	"*rahk*-tah-mah-lah"	Blood (Rakta) pure (Amala)
Swaasthya	"*swahs*-tee-yuh"	Self-dependence, self-contentment

The bija mantra Krim invokes the consciousness of Kali, a female form of Shiva—she rules the states of being inherent in the cycles of change.

When you recite the mantra, pay attention inside, simply sitting with yourself. You are completely self-contained, needing nothing other than your Self. Concentrate on your body, your heart, and your mind. Try to feel and observe the emotions that rise up, with the attitude of doing this as a gift for yourself. Find self-love if you can, or at least find self-sufficiency—self-trust or self-support. When emotions rise, integrate. Then go back to your meditation. *Please refer to the section on Swaasthya for a more complete teaching.*

~~~~~~~~~~~~~~~~~~~~~~~~~~~

See the Suggestions for Evaluation and Treatment at the end of the Level II section. There you will find more information about using these mantras, and also *how to take care of yourself before and after doing treatments.*

Esoteric Symbol Empowerment

Everything is made of consciousness. All the symbols that you draw naturally hold the consciousness infused by your intent to influence states of being. The Reiki symbols also hold the consciousness of Usui Sensei passed to you during your initiation, and Mahaananda Reiki teaches how you can give them even more power through the practice of Kuji-Kiri. Kuji-Kiri, an esoteric Buddhist tradition, is a form of spell casting used mainly for therapy. First you will empower your hands, and then use your empowered hands to empower a symbol. The final section presents the technique for empowering therapeutic tools.

Hand Empowerment

To empower your hand, you will do a 2-minute process involving focus and drawing. But before beginning, spend some time getting familiar with the Japanese kanji (Chinese characters) for Power, Hand, and Energy.

Ryoku (ree-*oh*-koo)	Te (tay)	Se-i (seh-ee)
Power	Hand	Spiritual Energy
力	手	精

The right hand signifies giving or projection, so this is the hand you will empower. Begin by making the sword mudra (holding ring and small finger with the thumb, and pointing with the index and major—like you did in the transmigration exercises). Gaze at your hand and transmigrate into it (imagine yourself inside it). Visualize your hand glowing with light, intensely condensing powerful energy. When you've got the feel of the energy, say "Ryoku Te Se-i" out loud while visualizing the kanji symbols in your hand.

Empowering the Hand

See the section below on "How to Draw Hand Empowerment Symbols" before proceeding.

Then, keeping your hand in the sword mudra, draw the symbols in the air in front of you, one over the other, knowing that you are drawing them into the substance of the universe. Visualize the symbols glowing with light when you draw them. Just before you are done drawing each symbol, say the corresponding Japanese word aloud. When you finish drawing the symbols, rest your right hand on your lap or in front of you, and focus again on the building up of energies in your hand.

Do this complete process of focus and drawing for 2 minutes, repeating at least 3 times, every day for 9 days in a row. You may empower the left hand each day after you have empowered the right, if you want to.

Symbol Empowerment

Now that your hand holds power, you will use it to empower the Reiki symbols that are presented in the Reiki Level II and Reiki Master sections of this book.

(Optional—If you want to draw the symbols with both hands, draw first with the right, then with the left each time you see "draw the symbol". Be sure to visualize that it is just the one symbol you are tracing twice, not two separate symbols.)

Step 1: Draw the symbol on paper (or look at a drawing) and meditate on the concept it represents. You want the *feeling* of the concept rather than the *thought* of it, so try not to use words.

Step 2: Draw the symbol once in the air in front of you using the sword mudra. Close your eyes and visualize it growing more and more powerful with radiant energy and light (use any color you want). Watch the symbol hovering in front of you for 10-15 seconds. Then see the symbol slowly move closer to you, and then enter your Third Eye chakra. It dissolves in your brain, then in your entire nervous system over a period of about 10-15 seconds. Recite the name of the symbol like a siddhi, slowly repeating it in your mind.

Draw the symbol a second time in front of you, powerful and radiant. Let it hover for 10-15 seconds, and then bring it slowly into your Solar Plexus chakra. Observe the symbol immerse your entire abdomen with its energy. Recite the name of the symbol again like a siddhi.

Draw the symbol a third time in front of you, powerful and radiant. Let it hover, then visualize the symbol growing larger and larger, and bring it into your entire body. Cover and fill your body with the energy of the symbol. Keep the name of the symbol like a siddhi in your mind.

Step 3: Meditate for at least 15 minutes on the energy and concept of the symbol, immersing yourself in the unworded feeling. Look at the symbol as much as you need to.

Do this empowerment meditation for 9 days per symbol.

Correct Brush Strokes

The next section displays Ryoku Te Se-i and a selection of other useful symbols, demonstrating the proper technique you will use for drawing them. The mindful effort of paying attention to correct strokes invests both your attention and intention in the empowerment process.

Remember that the Mahaananda Reiki body of wisdom only requires the use and empowerment of Ryoku Te Sei and the four original Reiki symbols. Refer to the Reiki Level II and III sections on Reiki Symbols for how to draw them, along with their meaning and uses. The other symbols included here—Mahaananda Reiki, the source kanji for the Reiki symbols, the five elements, and other helpful symbols—are presented for those of you who might find them very cool. You can use these symbols in therapy, in space clearing, or to infuse a state of being into a situation (or whatever else you can imagine).

How to Draw Hand Empowerment Symbols

Ryoku / Power

 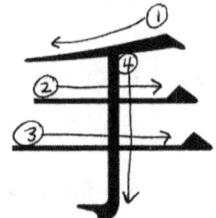

Te / Hand

 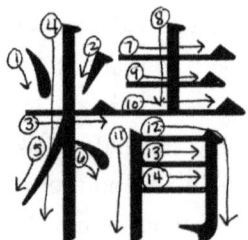

Se-i / Spiritual Energy

How to Draw "Mahaananda Reiki"

 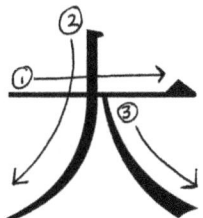

Maha (Great)

 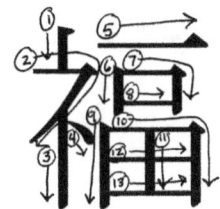

Ananda (Bliss)

 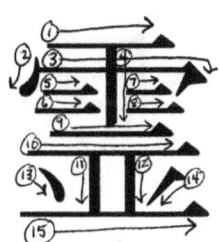

Rei (Spiritual, or Universal)

 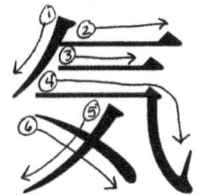

Ki (Nature, or Life Force Energy)

How to Draw the Source Kanji for Reiki Symbols

Hon Sha Ze Sho Nen Source Kanji

Hon 本　Sha 者　Ze 交　Sho 所　Nen 念

(Mostly visible and presented here are the Hon Sha Nen kanji.)

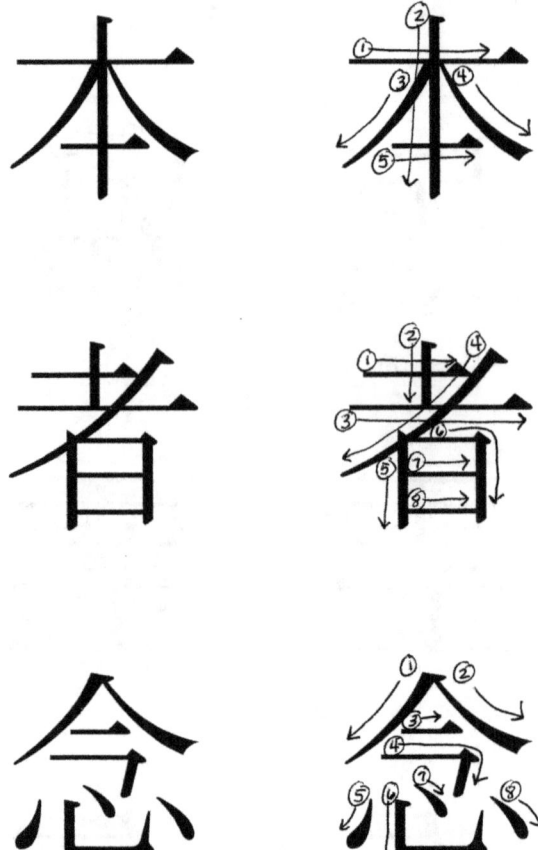

Dai Ko Myo Source Kanji

Dai 大   Ko 光   Myo 明

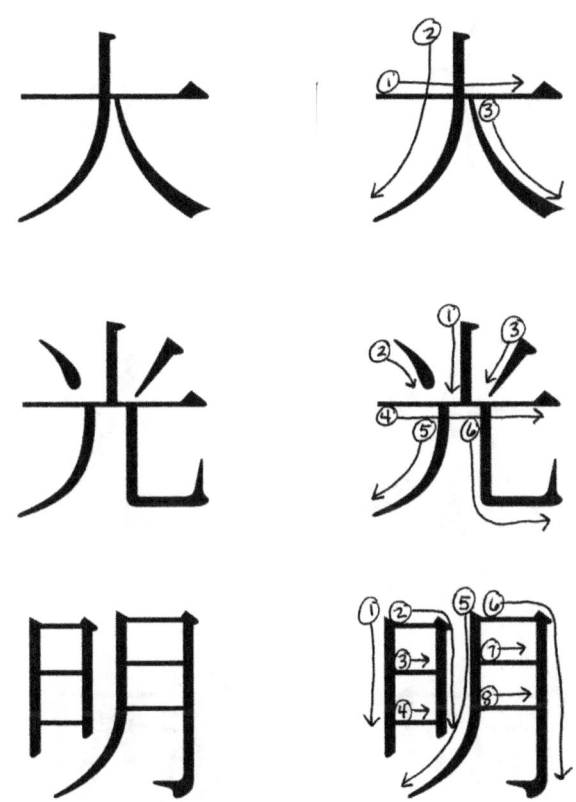

How to Draw the Five Elements Kanji

 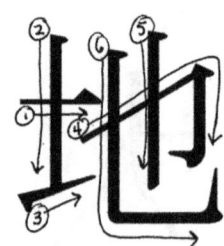

Chi / Earth

 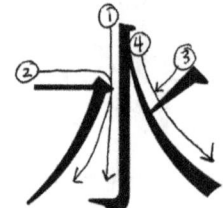

Sui / Water

 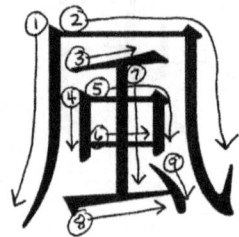

Fu / Wind, Air

Ka / Fire

 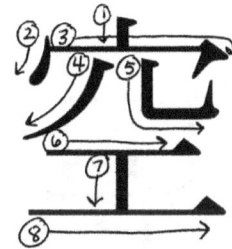

Ku / Void (Sky)

How to Draw Other Helpful Kanji

Ken / Health

 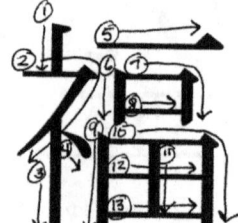

Fuku / Happiness

Tai / Peace

Ai / Love

Sha / Forgiveness

 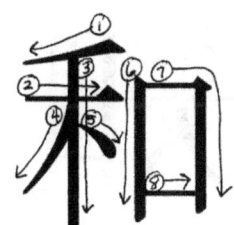

Wa / Harmony

同情

Dou Jou / Compassion (Same Feelings)

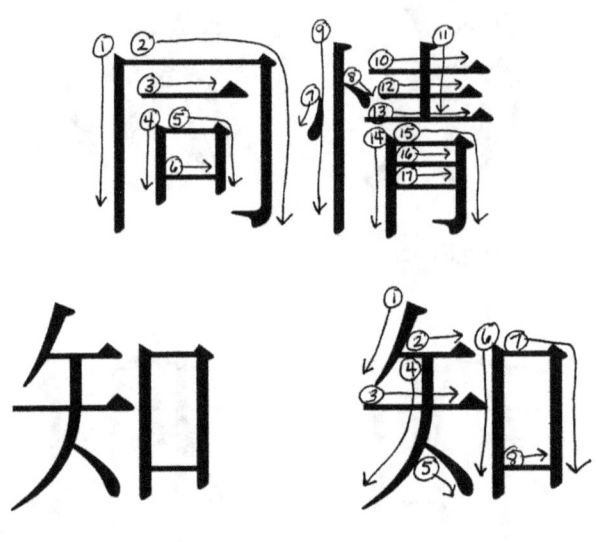

知

Chi / Wisdom

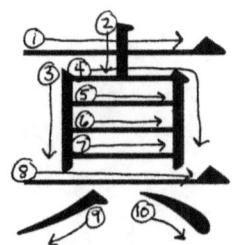

Shin / Truth

 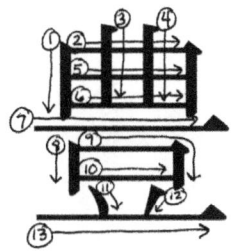

Ho-u / Abundance

 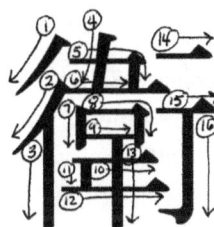

Ei / Protection

Raku (Lightning bolt)

Some Reiki traditions recognize Raku as a Reiki symbol—Mahaananda Reiki does not, but you can draw it as part of your treatment. Use this symbol to clear negative energy and cut through illusion. Draw it in the air with a quick forceful movement.

Tool Empowerment

Once your hand is empowered, you can use it to empower other tools such as crystals, bottles of essential oils, sage, or even get-well cards. The empowerment amplifies the inherent properties of the tool. Simply hold the object (or its container) in your right hand and visualize the radiant light of power and spiritual energy infusing the tools. Visualize the symbols (力精 Ryoku Se-i) in your empowered hand, radiating white light into the tool while the kanji symbols spiritually appear in the tool. This empowerment can take from a few moments to a few minutes.

Chakras, Soul and Evolution

You physically feel the human experience of chi, or vital energy, flowing and influencing your body and emotions (a result of physical hormones) as you meditate or receive energy work. So naturally it's easy to accept the common representation of the chakra—that it is as an empty funnel or vortex made of energy, and that the chakra system is something like a stream along which energy flows. I even teach it this way in Level I Reiki because it makes the concepts easier to grasp. But the chakra system is much more than this.

The chakra is the interaction of human and soul in the process of spiritual evolution. It is a kind of membrane, like a speaker in a sound system, through which consciousness and states of being resonate. It is a sensory "organ" of the soul which extends into your human existence, observing the human experiences of happiness and suffering, and at the same time radiating the lessons of the soul back to the human.

The following diagrams reflect the resonance of consciousness through the chakra—the simultaneous transmission and reception between human and spirit.

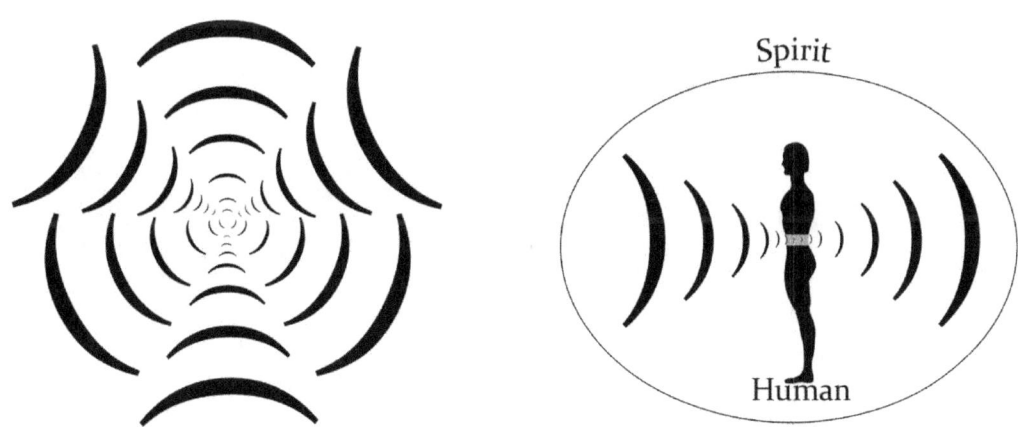

The resonance of each chakra vibrates at a frequency that corresponds to a particular type of evolutionary experience. It is our karma (these experiences), and our *resistance* to this karma that results in a group of associated mental, emotional and physical effects (see the section on The Meaning of Chakras in Level II Reiki).

REIKI TREATMENTS HELP RELAX OUR RESISTANCE TO LIFE EXPERIENCES.

Level II Reiki

About Reiki Level II

In the first level of Reiki you learned basic hand positions and what to look for in feeling energy in your treatment. That's all most people need or want to know; it's enough, along with initiation, to enable you to perform a good Reiki treatment.

Level II introduces the first three Reiki symbols. Remember that initiation of the symbols is the foundation of Usui Sensei's wisdom and consciousness. Actively using the symbols brings more focused power to your treatment and also assists you in doing distant treatments and infusing Reiki to inanimate objects. Level II also presents several advanced treatment techniques, as well as information about the association of each chakra with dis-ease. A Reiki treatment can be done without incorporating any of these things; but the wisdom and techniques do increase the efficiency of your work and bring you greater insight into the whole being of your client.

The Reiki Symbols

Introduction

The Reiki wisdom revealed to Usui Sensei during his enlightenment experience came in the form of four symbols and the consciousness inherent in each of them. The symbols themselves do not actually have names—we refer to each of them with a "jumon", which is a Japanese phrase (or spell) which describes its consciousness. Once you are initiated, the consciousness of the symbols lives inside you and awakens the transformational abilities discussed in the initiation section of this book. Some traditions of Reiki include additional symbols, such as Raku or Antakharana—I received a Violet Flame Reiki initiation that taught 40 symbols! But Mahaananda Reiki recognizes only the four that Usui Sensei taught (three in Reiki Level II and the fourth in the Master Level) and requires you to personally empower them as explained in the section on Esoteric Symbol Empowerment.

- A Reiki Master Teacher uses the symbols to create a Reiki practitioner through initiation.
- Level II Reiki-ists invoke the consciousness of the symbols to intensify therapy (with the first two symbols); and also, to work at a level more subtle than the human structure of time and space—the ability to do treatments to a far-away person, in the past or future, or to an inanimate object.

For many years the symbols were kept secret to prevent misuse and disrespect—only Reiki masters and Level II practitioners knew them. However, the more modern view is that the symbols are sacred, but not secret, and you can learn about the symbols almost anywhere. But the consciousness is received only through initiation.

Invoking the Symbols

You can invoke the consciousness of the symbols by thinking the "name" of the symbol or saying it out loud. You can also use the image of the symbol by drawing it or visualizing it. You could draw it on paper, in the air, with your fingers or palm on a person or thing, on the roof of your mouth with your tongue, as part of a walking meditation, or even with your steps in a martial arts style (like we did at Sigung's Xen academy). Some schools of thought require the name of the symbol to be spoken three times after drawing them.

Drawing and Memorizing the Symbols

When drawing symbols and kanji freestyle, each person's drawing style can be a bit different—like writing a word in cursive. So while there is not a perfect and official way to draw them, do your best to copy the following images as you use the proper brushstrokes.

It is not absolutely required to memorize the symbols, but I highly recommend it. Imagine yourself giving a treatment. You decide to use a symbol, so you must remove at least one hand from your client, shift your intent from your client to a piece of paper, which your client also notices. How did this feel? Your level of consciousness most likely dropped. I am saying these things from experience—I didn't force myself to memorize the symbols until I gave my first initiation, but I hope for better experiences for you.

The Meaning of the First Two Symbols

Usui Sensei received the images of the symbols and their names. In a kanji dictionary, you will find a lot of Japanese words that sound the same but have different kanji, and then different meanings for each of the kanji. Because for the first two symbols we have an image and a spoken name but no actual kanji to reference, there are various interpretations being taught in different Reiki traditions. Mahaananda Reiki uses two interpretations each for Choku Rei and Sei Hei Ki—one that addresses primarily the level of nature (mind, heart and body), and one that addresses primarily the level of soul (evolution). **In Mahaananda Reiki, use both intentions in your therapy in order to affect both Nature and Soul.**

Practical Application of the Symbols

General information regarding practical application of each of the first three symbols is presented below. For specific therapeutic examples see the section on Combining Reiki II and Spiritual Techniques. Remember that performing the symbol empowerment process will bring the most power to your use of the symbols—I drew these symbols presented here after empowering my hands and the symbols.

First Reiki Symbol—Choku Rei

(Pronounced "choh-koo-*ray*")

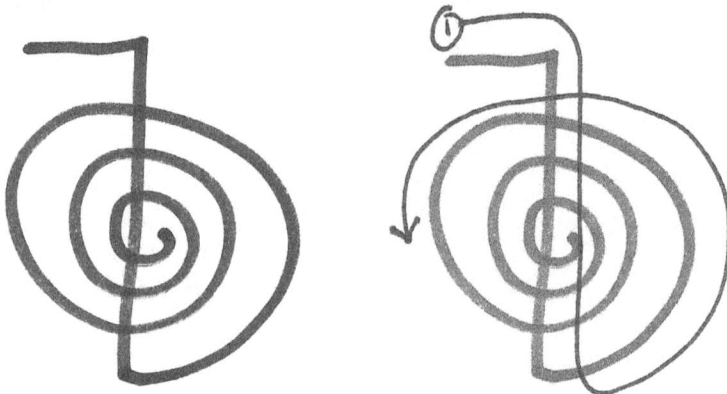

The common Nature interpretation of Choku Rei is "the direct and immediate intervention of the spirit". From this perspective, the image reflects tangible consciousness moving into a chakra (beginning from the top left of the symbol, then moving down and spiraling in). The Japanese word Choku Rei seems too similar to the Sanskrit word "Chakra" to be coincidental, since many Japanese spiritual writings (including the Heart Sutra and Kuji-In mantras) phonetically mimic the original Sanskrit versions.

See below that the first symbol from the esoteric Soul interpretation (Cho Kuu Rei) represents Kundalini energy. Kundalini is consciousness (in the form of a spiral wrapped tightly 3 ¼ times on itself) which results from divine incarnation, residing in the Base chakra. When awakened during evolution, kundalini releases the pressure of its tight hold over itself and rises up the spine, up and over the head, and out of the 3rd Eye chakra. The first symbol reflects this release of Kundalini energy (beginning from the center of the symbol, then up and out).

Kanji (*information for interpretation only—use the symbol above for therapy*):

Nature Interpretation			Soul Interpretation		
Choku:	直	Direct/ immediate	Cho:	緒	String binding soul
Rei:	霊	Spirit	Kuu:	空	Void, fifth element
			Rei:	霊	Spirit

Practical Applications of Choku Rei

Choku Rei is the Power Symbol—the common meaning is Open the Gate, or Put the Power Here. It primarily addresses the physical nature of things.

- Use it to begin each of your treatments.
- Use it at the end of each of your treatments to seal in the therapy.
- Use it to focus more energy at specific chakras or other areas where needed.
- Use it along with the second symbol to add to the second symbol's power—draw Choku Rei first, then Sei Hei Ki.
- Use it for all physical ailments, such as injury and disease.
- Use it for purification or energy cleansing—such as cleansing your treatment room of negative energy, or purifying your food (although I prefer to bless food rather than Reiki it).
- Use it for protection—such as drawing it on your car before a road trip, or drawing it on yourself to protect from energy vampires (people who are drawn to *and drain* the radiance of others).
- Use it to ground yourself and feel more connected to your body.
- Use it to infuse Reiki into inanimate objects (see the section on Infusing Inanimate Objects with Reiki).

And from the soul perspective of Cho Kuu Rei, the intent is to help you or your client relax resistance to evolutionary experiences, allowing kundalini to rise.

Second Reiki Symbol—Sei Hei Ki

(Pronounced "say-*hay*-key")

Hrih

Sei Hei Ki was inspired by a Sanskrit symbol, the HRIH seed mantra of purification. This stylized version of Hrih represents a person facing left. The line on the right is the spine and back. The top horizontal part of this line is the shoulders, which carrying the inner weight of our life's burdens; the two small arcs represent emanations from the Heart and Solar Plexus chakras. The left, or inner line, begins at the base of the Throat chakra, peeks at the Heart, then peeks again with more weight at the Solar Plexus. It then descends softly, relaxing at the level of the Sacral chakra.

Sei Hei Ki soothes mental and emotional ailments and loosens the hold we have on our habits. When written Sei Heiki, this symbol speaks of a spiritual state of being of composure and nonconcern—the enlightened state of non-expectation and non-attachment.

Kanji (*information for interpretation only—use the symbol above for therapy*):

Nature Interpretation

Sei: 正 Rectify, purify

Hei: 病 Illness

Ki: 気 Mind / heart / mood

Soul Interpretation

Sei: 聖 Spiritual, holy or sacred

Heiki: 平気 Composure; nonconcern

Practical Applications of Sei Hei Ki

Sei Hei Ki is the Mental/Emotional Symbol—the common meaning is Emotional Composure, or Create a New Habit.

- Use it to purify and soothe emotions.
- Use it to treat depression.
- Use it to empower the heart, bringing confidence.
- Use it to bring love and forgiveness for yourself and your relationships.
- Use it to purify and soothe thoughts.
- Use it to balance the right and left sides of the brain, bringing harmony and peace.
- Use it to help relax or break habits.
- Use it to improve mental perception and thought process.
- Use it to improve memory, and to make study and learning sessions more efficient.
- Use it to treat emotional or physical yearning (addictions and desires) and pain.
- Use it to treat physical problems that are the result of mental or emotional suffering. I *always* use it along with Choku Rei to treat physical ailments.

And from the soul perspective of Sei Heiki, the intent is to help you or your client let go of expectations and attachments, which naturally brings enlightenment.

Third Reiki Symbol—Hon Sha Ze Sho Nen

(Pronounced "hone-shah- zay-shoh-nen")

 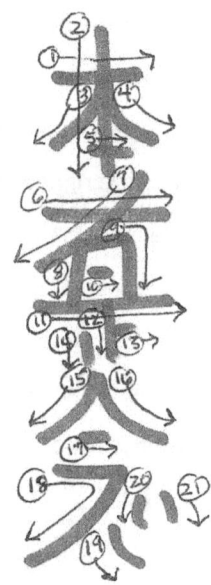

The only meaning and power of the third symbol is to intersect dimensions—to make your presence real in another place or time and do distant therapy. There are many explanations about the uses of this symbol, such as: allowing access to Akashic records, repairing the aura, changing the cellular make-up of the body, and even dissolving karmic debt. But anything not directly related to its original meaning did not come from Usui Sensei.

Kanji (*information for interpretation only—use the symbol above for therapy*):

Hon:	本	Real / reality
Sha:	者	Person
Ze:	交	Intersect
Sho:	所	Place
Nen:	念	Feeling

The Reiki symbol for Hon Sha Ze Sho Nen comes from this kanji series, but is artistically altered (stylized) to make it faster to write. Mostly visible are the Hon Sha Nen kanji, which means "Real person feeling".

Practical Applications of Hon Sha Ze Sho Nen

Hon Sha Ze Sho Nen is the Spiritual Symbol—the common meaning is Everything Comes from Man's Heart and Mind (from Lao Xie); or Correct Mindfulness is the Essence of Being. We use it only to facilitate distant treatments. For me, transmigration is much more powerful and versatile than the third symbol. However, Sho Nen (Sigung taught us to use "Sho Nen" as a shortened nickname for this symbol) can be helpful to the therapist that uses visualization to assist in "opening the door".

See the upcoming sections on methods for using Sho Nen.

- Use it to do Reiki therapy on distant people, places or things (that are not right in front of you).
- Use it to treat life-changing past emotional trauma.
- Use it for protection and therapy in future events.

How to Use Sho Nen—Treating Outside the Limitation of Time and Space

Should you get permission from your client before doing a treatment that crosses space and/or time? This is a treatment they may or may not know about. Some traditions believe it's absolutely required to get permission, or else there could be unpleasant karmic repercussions for the therapist. In Mahaananda Reiki it's not required to ask first. Sigung taught that everyone (at some level) wants to be healthier and happier. So if you cannot make contact with your client, or you want to do the therapy without telling them, just do it with the intent that if they want to accept it, they will; and if they don't want to accept it, they won't. Maha teaches that there are karmic repercussions for helping someone—but it's "good" karma.

It might be hard to believe before you experience it, but you will probably feel more sensation during distant treatments than in-person treatments—both I and almost all of my local students do. And please do get feedback from your client; it's important for your training and also to build your confidence.

My first experience doing a distant treatment was working on a friend who lived in the snowy mountains of New Mexico. She was having a very painful bout of fibromyalgia and also couldn't get warm or fall asleep—along with her treatment I Reiki-ed her blankets. Her pain level decreased, she began to feel warm, and was finally able to drift off. (See the section on Infusing Inanimate Objects with Reiki.)

Connecting to Your Client with Sho Nen

To do a distant treatment, follow the steps for any treatment (see the following section on How to Do a Reiki Treatment Using Symbols and Mantras). Before you begin, gently connect with your client using either transmigration or by drawing Sho Nen. If you are drawing Sho Nen, you can use physical objects or images to represent your client if it's helpful, such as:

- A picture of your client (a cell phone picture is fine—and this is very helpful for transmigration as well)
- An object that belongs to your client (piece of jewelry or clothing, a favorite book)
- A stuffed animal or doll (which represents the body of your client)
- Your body (for example, treat YOUR knee when working on a client who had a knee replacement surgery)
- Imagine the person sitting or lying in front of you, as a physical body or as an aura. Visualize moving and repositioning the body easily, so that you can comfortably reach whatever area you want to treat. I prefer this method in my therapy.

Method for Treating the Manifestations of Past Trauma

Someone might have experienced a traumatic event (such as rape or the death of a parent) 20 years ago and didn't know how to resolve their suffering. Past suffering flavors the way we perceive life and relationships from that point forward. What if you could transcend time and use Reiki to help them relax their resistance to the experience, helping to soothe their life?

Using the Distant Treatment method, visualize the past traumatic event and your client's reaction to this event (obviously this requires a pre-session discussion). Use the Sei Hei Ki symbol to soothe the pain at the time of the event, to foster emotional strength to carry forward, and to loosen attachment to the suffering associated with the experience.

Method for Protection and Therapy in Future Events

Using the Distant Treatment method, visualize a future event, such as an upcoming surgery, an impending death, or a road trip. For surgeries, I Reiki the operating room equipment, all medical workers (these folks have to work when they are upset or don't feel well) and the patient. I used Sho Nen and Choku Rei on my son and his car when he was taking off on a cross-country road trip. Use the Choku Rei symbol for power and physical protection, and the Sei Hei Ki symbol for emotional protection.

How to Do a Reiki Treatment Using Symbols and Mantras

When I refer below to drawing or visualizing a symbol, I mean to draw it into your client. You can imagine a piece of paper resting flat on the body or at the aura (the "sweet spot" where you feel the cushion of energy). Your finger is drawing onto that paper, but the symbol is appearing, or manifesting, inside the body. (And of course, this "drawing" can be done in your mind—you don't have to use imaginary paper.)

Preparation

- Sometime during the day on which you will do Reiki therapy, consciously reconnect to the energies of the Elements by reciting each mantra. For personal preparation and protection, do a few recitations or one mala of each mantra.

- Prepare to use your mantras by increasing the awareness of them inside you. If you have already completed the charging of the mantras, this could be done with a brief contemplation. If you haven't yet completed the charging, contemplate and recite the mantras 9 times.

- Wash your hands for good hygiene, and also as symbolic of purification.

- Acknowledge the gift and guidance of Usui Sensei, Sigung and Maha—meditate or contemplate to feel their consciousness.

- Pay attention inside yourself—be aware of your own body and state of being. The Compassion or Peaceful Soul mantras can help you sink into yourself.

- Open yourself to service with love. Release any expectations or attachment to the outcome of your treatment. "God, may Thy will be done"

Treatment

- Transmigrate into your client. If it's a distant treatment, either transmigrate or connect with your client using Sho Nen (see the previous section on Connecting to Your Client with Sho Nen).

- Draw or visualize Choku Rei to "open the door", saying the name aloud or silently. Draw it either large to cover the head and torso; or at the Heart chakra, visualizing it emanating through the head and torso.

- Do your therapy, using hand positions, symbols and mantras. Remember that the Reiki aspect of the therapy just flows because you act as a conduit. However, when using mantras, you purposely invoke the therapeutic power of a state of being.

    o Draw Choku Rei and Sei Hei Ki as needed at each chakra or area of the body, saying the name aloud or silently. "As needed" is up to you. It could be to just draw them each once with the intent that the body and heart take what is needed, or to draw both of them on each major chakra. It could be that you use what you know about your client's issues along with the information in the section on The Physical and Emotional/Experiential Associations of Chakras. It could be using your intuition, or a combination of all of these choices.

- o After you draw a symbol, place your hands over the chakra and recite any mantras (aloud or silently) that work well with the symbol and with the experience of your client: Peace, Compassion, Three Suns, Earth, Fire, Water, Air, Peaceful Soul, or any of the Well-being mantras. See the following section on Pairing Mantras with Reiki Symbols.

- Simply wait to feel the change. From the Reiki aspect, you are looking for gentle warmth or vibration (or however you experience energy), the same intensity at all the chakras. From the Spiritual Techniques point of view, also wait for the feeling that the negative emotion of your client is relaxing and transforming.

  These are not two separate steps; it is one combined experience. The vibration might become to feel like emotion, and the emotion like vibration, until it is all the same thing. This advanced level of perception will come with time and practice.

- Seal the treatment by drawing a final Choku Rei—either large to cover the head and torso; or at the Heart chakra, visualizing it emanating through the head and torso.

Closing

- Feel and express gratitude for the opportunity to be in service by making Reiki therapy available to your client (or to yourself for a self-treatment). Bow to your client with prayer hands.

- After each treatment, purify yourself by washing your hands with cool water and meditating a short while.

  - o If you did Reiki only, and you are not an empath, there is no additional personal purification to do. If you are an empath (you tend to take on the emotional or even physical suffering of others), follow the recommendation in the next bullet.

  - o If you transmigrate to do mantras, some amount of your client's ailments might affect you. Chant a few of the Elemental mantras, Peace, Compassion, and Three Suns mantras (the ones which you have charged) for yourself after the treatment to purify your own energies and get back to a pure state of being. Always do more for yourself than you did for your client. If you continue to feel the emotions of your client, do emotional integration.

- Your final spiritual practice should be stillness meditation. Sit still in a comfortable way, with eyes completely or partially closed, and pay attention to your breath. Recite the single word Swaasthya ("*swah*-stee-yuh") every few seconds, either softly or silently. Center your attention inside, only on yourself, without any other goal than to be with yourself—self-dependent and self-content (see the Swaasthya teaching in the Master section for more complete instructions). Meditate from 5 minutes to 1 hour.

Using Mantras for Therapy

What is the difference between using elemental mantras versus well-being mantras? For example, to treat a bacterial infection should you use Water and Fire, or the Purification of the Body mantra?

The elemental mantras are a general resource or support for both you as the therapist and for your client. The body knows what to do with them, so your attention doesn't need to be specific (like Reiki). The well-being mantras are mechanical in nature and meant for specific ailments. If you are only going to use one type of mantra, use the elemental mantras as they are more powerful. The well-being mantras work on their own, but work best as fine tuning along with the elements.

While doing therapy and chanting elemental or "other" mantras, place your attention either in the entire body/emotional experience of your client, or in an individual chakra. If using well-being mantras, pay attention to the specific ailment or emotional experience.

Here is a quick reference of the general beneficial properties of mantras. It is not a complete list, just the most common examples.

Elemental Mantras:

- Earth—regeneration of damaged organs or bones; condition stabilizer; protection from harm, infection, or energy vampires; support for mental health (being grounded)
- Fire—inflammation; bacterial and viral infection; tumor treatment; raising the general physical energy level
- Heaven—*used for raising your own consciousness, but not for treating others. It's more of a blessing for yourself.*
- Water—any problem having to do with fluids, such as liver, kidney, bladder, stomach, lymph, hormones or blood problems; transportation of nutrients needed to assist regeneration or energy increase; soothing effect on physical pain or a broken heart; relaxation of a controlling personality. Use both fire and water to boil and cleanse impurities like bacteria.
- Air—aid in communication, in mental agility and clarity, and balance; assist information to flow through the nervous system

Other Mantras:

- Peace—calms the mind and body, bringing relief from worry, anxiety, anger
- Compassion—calms the heart, reducing the feeling of separation and judgment
- Three Suns—increases energy levels (be careful here—If someone is angry, this mantra could increase the anger)
- Peaceful Soul—brings happiness and peace, and is very helpful for depression; increases your or your client's awareness of their own soul (refer to the section on The Peaceful Soul—additional charging must be done in order to most efficiently treat your client)

Well-Being Mantras:

- Purification of the Body—purifies the effects of infection, parasites, drugs, smoking, cholesterol
- Regeneration of the Body—helps recovery from physical injury or degeneration; post-surgery recovery
- Soothing Emotional Wounds—helps with emotional trauma, such as death of a loved one, divorce, Post Traumatic Stress Disorder
- Clearing Negative Thinking/Positive Thinking—helps bring a feeling that everything will be fine; grows faith; empowers manifestation, helps with procrastination
- Chemical Dependency Purification Mantra—helps to stop drinking, smoking, taking drugs, eating sugar, etc.

Some Examples:

- Treating mental conditions: Use the Earth element with your right thumb at the third eye, thumb pointing down, to bring a grounding experience to the mind. (Someone who is down to earth usually does not have mental illness.) Then use well-being mantras per your intuition.
- Treating depression: Soothe the heart with the Soothing Emotional Wounds mantra, then the negativity with the Clearing Negative Thinking mantra, and then use the Earth mantra to ground.
- Addictions: Use the CDPM to purify the body and clear negativity. This will not release addictions and dependencies to substances unless you or your client does integration, or at least faces the suffering attached to it.

Pairing Mantras with Reiki Symbols

As a general guideline, mantras which primarily affect the physical body (such as the Five Elements, Three Suns, or Regeneration of the Body) work well with the first Reiki symbol. Mantras which primarily affect the mind and heart (such as Peace, Peaceful Soul, Compassion, or Soothing Emotional Wounds) work well with the second symbol. The Chemical Dependency Purification Mantra works with both the body and heart, so use both the first and second symbols.

The Physical and Emotional/Experiential Associations of Chakras

All you really need in order to be a Reiki therapist is the initiation; and in order to do a Reiki treatment you simply place your hands over the chakras and wait for the sense of balance. Knowing what it might mean when a particular chakra is not balanced isn't necessary to perform the treatment, but it is important for guiding your client (or yourself) in caring for their own physical, emotional and mental health. A physical dis-ease is a manifestation of mental or emotional dis-ease and reminds us to go inside and observe ourselves, with compassion and forgiveness. Gently guide and encourage your client to do emotional integration if you feel she is open to it.

The emotional, mental and physical associations with the eight major chakras, and also the Yong Quan and the Dan-Tian, are presented below. The spiritual lesson or experience underlies the associated issues (see the section on Chakras, Soul and Evolution). The chakra associations are not mutually exclusive to the chakras as I've shown in the very structured boxes below—the "border" that separates each chakra from the others is a non-defined, blended transition.

Base/Root Chakra and Yong Quan *(at sole of the foot)* *survival and grounding* *"I am"* *The spiritual lesson comes from allowing faith to overcome fear.*	
<u>Mental/Emotional/Experiential</u>	<u>Physical</u>
• Survival (money/home/job) • Physical security, stability, safety and trust (tribe or community) • Grounding • Desire for life or death <u>Balanced</u>: feeling of being well-supported; confidence in easily meeting basic needs (ability to draw abundance from the planet) <u>Imbalanced</u>: difficulty achieving goals; things that are not urgent or important can cause anxiety and worry; decisions can be difficult; stubbornness; depression; greed; feeling uprooted or unsupported	• Sacral Plexus • Adrenal glands (Fight or Flight response) • Lymphatic system • Elimination system (large intestine and colon) • Skeletal system Examples are osteoarthritis, spine problems (slipped disk, sciatic pain, scoliosis), and lymphatic difficulties; birth and rebirth. <u>Yong Quan</u> (soles of the feet) Indicates overall energetic health

Sacral Chakra *"Water chakra"*
change, sexuality and creativity, emotions
"I feel"
The spiritual lesson comes from allowing self-mastery to overcome karma*.

Mental/Emotional/Experiential	Physical
<ul><li>Accepting or adjusting to change</li><li>Emotional security</li><li>Creativity (procreation and artistic)</li><li>Acceptance of pleasure</li><li>Feeling comfortable with ones' sexuality</li></ul>**Balanced**: feeling cared for and nurtured by life, loved ones, and self; healthy sexual desire; healthy balance of internal and external sources of happiness; yin and yang (the masculine and feminine aspects of our personality) are flowing and in balance; creative expression is effortless; enthusiasm for life **Imbalanced**: unhealthy appetite for outside comforts—food, sex, drugs, electronics, shopping, gambling, material things—in misguided attempt to feel cared for (or to distract from not feeling cared for); difficulty enjoying life; unfulfilling relationships; emotional distress; rigidity; overly yielding	<ul><li>Lumbar plexus</li><li>Reproductive system/glands</li><li>Urinary system (kidney/bladder)</li><li>Prostate</li><li>Lower back</li></ul>Examples are infertility; bladder or kidney infections; sexual dysfunction or lack of sexual desire; addictions, low back pain.

* Karma is the current life experience which results from past actions, words, and thoughts.

Solar Plexus Chakra and Dan-Tian*
will and power (self-esteem)   *"I do"*   The spiritual lesson of the Dan-Tian comes from allowing self-observation to overcome drama; the spiritual lesson of the Solar Plexus comes from allowing kindness and humility to master power.

Mental/Emotional/Experiential	Physical
- Sense of personal power - Emotions of power—joy and anger Balanced: healthy sense of self identity; self-confidence and self-esteem; assertiveness (standing up for yourself or your beliefs); self-control; will power; charisma; successful transformation of ideas into action (career); happy and joyful Imbalanced: aggressive; confrontational; feels the need to be "right"; frustration; feels ineffectual; overly passive; overly sensitive to criticism; easily intimidated; depression; sadness; frequent mood swings	- Solar plexus - Stomach/digestive system (from mouth through small intestine) - Liver - Pancreas (production and interaction of insulin) - Gall bladder - Spleen - Muscle system - Energy Examples are the conversion of energy to physical form (digestive difficulties), fatigue, diabetes, mid-back pain.

* Chi is gathered and stored in the Dan-Tian for use by the body.

Heart Chakra
love and compassion
"I love"
The spiritual lesson comes from allowing compassion to overcome attachment to identity.

Mental/Emotional/Experiential	Physical
<ul><li>Love</li><li>Compassion</li><li>Empathy</li><li>Healing</li></ul>Balanced: unification—connection and relation to others; warm-heartedness; sympathy; easily gives and receives; devotion; sense of well-being Imbalanced: alienation from others; unhealthy competition; comparison and judgment; hatred; cruelty; inability to feel, express or accept love and compassion for self and others; overly compassionate; commitment and betrayal issues; front of the chakra affected by others and back affected by self (perfectionist); grief The Heart chakra has a great influence on all other chakras.	<ul><li>Cardiac plexus</li><li>Heart and circulatory system</li><li>Lungs and respiratory system</li><li>Thymus gland (produces hormones that support the immune system)</li></ul>Examples are circulation problems (high blood pressure, blood clots, heart disease), breathing problems (asthma, COPD), chronic illness, upper back pain. These physical systems are very affected by stress.

Throat Chakra
communication and forgiveness
"I speak, I listen"
The spiritual lesson comes from allowing communication at the soul level—simply aware of what causes happiness and what causes suffering—to dissolve our own opinions.

Mental/Emotional/Experiential	Physical
<ul><li>Expression (in all layers of communication)</li><li>Forgiveness</li></ul>Balanced: can express one's self with safety and confidence; listens and speaks honestly and compassionately to others (can be poets, authors, song-writers); in tune with the inner voice and balances it well with external communication Imbalanced: doesn't feel heard; unable to express messages for fear of conflict or hurt feelings; overly communicative; not being in tune (or spending too much time) with the inner voice; holds grudges	<ul><li>Cervical plexus</li><li>Throat</li><li>Neck</li><li>Vocal apparatus</li><li>Thyroid (produces hormones that regulate metabolism and growth)</li></ul>Examples are physical maturity and other thyroid issues (growth, metabolism), sore throat, chronic neck pain.

Third Eye and Jade Gate Chakras
vision
"I see"
The spiritual experience of the 3rd Eye is creation at the divine level—with no expectation or attachment; the spiritual experience of the Jade Gate is perception at the divine level—beneath the veil of space and time.

Mental/Emotional/Experiential	Physical
3rd Eye - Clarity and purity of mind - Analytical thinking - Manifestation - Dreaming Balanced: clear and focused mind; good analytical skills; good memory; expanded imagination; ability to draw experiences (manifestation); trusts inner guidance; has clear sense of purpose Imbalanced: self-doubt and distrust; refusal to accept what one is seeing; over-dependence on the intellect; low intellect level; clouded judgment; delusions; illusions (over-involved in fantasy or imagination) ~~~~~~~~~~~~~~~~~~~~~~~~ Jade Gate - Supernatural Perception (beyond the five senses) Balanced: ability to see through the illusion of time and space; insight; intuition; clairvoyance, clairaudience and remote viewing; individualized consciousness Imbalanced: little or no supernatural perception	**3rd Eye** - Carotid plexus - Pituitary and hypothalamus glands (the pituitary gland is referred to as the "master gland")—together these two glands regulate the entire endocrine system (all hormone-producing glands) - Lower skull/brain - Eyes - Nose - Ears - Sinuses Examples are hormonal imbalances; poor vision, headaches, sinus infections, poor hearing; vertigo; unrestful sleep; nightmares. ~~~~~~~~~~~~~~~~~~~~~~~~~~ Jade Gate - Lower brain - Jaw - Some effect on shoulders and upper back Examples are poor dental health, TMJ, salivary gland issues

Crown Chakra *spirituality* *"I understand"* *The spiritual experience is awareness of personal universal divinity.*	
<u>Mental/Emotional/Experiential</u> - Universal Consciousness - Spiritual evolution Balanced: glimpses (or more often) of divine perception of being, such as personal divinity and that everything exists in the Self—individuality melts into universality; trusting evolution (open-ness, understanding, and gratitude of all spiritual experience and growth) Imbalanced: sense of separation, abandonment and being lost; mistaken sense of personal enlightenment (closing off to spiritual growth); lack of direction; lack of spirituality The Crown chakra has a great influence on all other chakras.	<u>Physical</u> - Cerebral cortex - Central nervous system - Upper skull/brain Examples are epilepsy, Alzheimer's, any kind of pain, fibromyalgia.

Infusing Inanimate Objects with Reiki

You can infuse any object with Reiki so that it continues to radiate energy to your client after your Reiki treatment is over, rather like an energetic time-release capsule. The variety of objects you might choose is limited only by your own imagination—here are a few examples of things I have Reiki-ed:

- A sofa pillow to put behind the back for back pain
- A pillow on which to rest a broken leg
- A bed pillow to assist with sleeping problems
- A blanket for chronic body pain (arthritis or fibromyalgia)
- A blanket to speed recovery from surgery
- Personal objects—jewelry, glasses, or a doll held by a sick child

The pillow for the broken leg was actually the first experience I had with infusing inanimate objects. Remember my friend that had the car accident and came to the Xen academy to receive group therapy? She was in danger of having a foot amputated—she had lost a large area of skin around her crushed ankle and the skin grafts weren't working. I asked Sigung to help, and he met us at her house. Here he did therapy and also asked for the pillow that she rested the ankle on. I watched him infuse the pillow with Reiki, then asked him later how to do it. My friend made a complete physical recovery other than her ankle being a bit stiff, and not being able to wear high heels anymore.

Method for Infusing Inanimate Objects with Reiki

Draw Choku Rei on or over the object. With your hands in a hands-off position, transmit Reiki energy to the object until it's "full"—when you feel it pushing back a little. Then visualize a golden light covering the object and lower both hands to rest them on the object—this seals in the energy. The energy generally lasts a few days to a week, depending on how quickly your or your client's body draws it in. To do this from a distance, begin with transmigration or Sho Nen.

Blessing Objects

Although many people Reiki these types of objects, my personal opinion is that it is more appropriate to bless them. To bless the object, put your hands around it. It's not necessary to touch it, but it's up to you. Transmigrate into the object and bring yourself into the state of being you want to use for the blessing—Gratitude or Peace are great possibilities—using a method such as contemplation, prayer, or mantra. Then when you use or ingest the objects, you (or your client) receive the blessing.

- Spiritual objects—any altar object such as statues, incense, stones and crystals; or crucifixes, saint medallions and malas
- Food—transform the negative emotion in meat, poultry, or fish released upon the death of the animal, or the harmful effects of hormones
- Herbs and Medicines

Additional Techniques

Scanning

The Level I basic technique is to proceed through all of the hand positions, spending additional time as needed when you sense an imbalance or blockage. Scanning techniques allow you to quickly identify the most "out of balance" areas before you begin treatment. You can use this information to have a conversation with your client about what her energetic state is trying to tell her (see the previous section on The Physical and Emotional/Experiential Associations of Chakras). Scanning can help you do a more efficient treatment—if you don't have much time, you can treat just these areas. Because the work you do with each chakra affects all chakras to some extent, it's possible that a chakra that you felt sure was balanced during the treatment might have shifted a bit. So scan again at the end of a treatment—you might find a little fine-tuning you need to do.

Scanning with your Palms

- Begin at the crown, leaving your hands there just long enough to feel the intensity of vibration (or however you experience the feel of energy). I usually use only my left hand as it is more sensitive than my right hand.
- Then move through all of the energy gates, spending only a few moments at each one as you compare the intensity of vibration between all of them.

Sigung taught some of the following techniques, and others came from my own intuition. Try them all out, use the ones you like, and be open to your own intuition to discover others.

Scanning with a Pendulum

Expert pendulum practitioners use beautiful pendulums made of powerful stones or crystals which they have spent time training with so that it will answer questions. Sigung taught us a very simplified technique using a makeshift pendulum. A pendulum doesn't have to be fancy—all you need is a string or light chain (like a necklace), with a weight at the bottom that can easily spin. My current pendulum is an American flag medallion I took off an old keychain which I then attached to the end of an old cheap necklace chain. One day I will get myself a nicer one, but this one works just fine.

- Hold your pendulum by wrapping the free end of the chain around the fingers of the hand you will be using to scan. Then secure the chain by pressing it against your palm with those fingers. The chain should hang about 4 inches below your hand.

- Beginning with the Crown, hold the pendulum a few inches above each of the chakras for a few moments (if your client is lying down). If she is sitting, hold the pendulum in front of the chakras. You are observing both the movement pattern of the pendulum—back and forth, in a clockwise circle, in a counterclockwise circle, or no movement at all—and the speed of the movement.
- When the pendulum moves differently at one or several chakras than it does for most of the others, that indicates an imbalance.

Muscle Testing

- Have your client sit or stand with their dominant arm held at shoulder level out to the side of the body.
- Test the natural buoyant resistance of the arm muscle by pressing lightly on the outstretched hand, releasing the pressure immediately. Guide your client to use the amount of strength that will allow her arm to be moved down an inch or two, and then pop back up as soon as you release pressure.
- Now with one of your hands held above the Crown chakra, test the buoyant resistance as in the previous bullet point. Do this with each of the other chakras, holding the "chakra" hand a few inches in front or behind your client.
- Identify which chakras produce more or less resistance than in the original "general" muscle test—either weaker or more rigid. This indicates a need for treatment.

Follow the Energy

- With your hands at the Crown chakra,
- Close your eyes, and give the energy a thickish fluid consistency (like paint) and a bright color of your choosing. I like green.
- With your 3rd Eye, follow the flow of color from your client's Crown chakra through her entire body, until it flows out of the Yong Quan (soles of the feet).
- Look for areas where the flow is not smooth, or the color changes—which indicates a need for treatment. Problems in areas such as organs and bones might reveal themselves with this technique.
    - It doesn't flow at all
    - It seems to get clogged up
    - It's flowing, but not "solid"—it appears to have bubbles or holes
    - It appears to change color (to a darker color, or black)

Test the Heart Chakra and Listen with Your Entire Body

When I first began my Reiki practice in 2006, I rented a small room in the office of a massage therapist. This room tended to be chilly, and my cold hands found it difficult to sense the energy. The same thing happens if air conditioning or heating is blowing across my hands. I had to pay very close attention to be aware of energy, and began to notice that I felt energy in other parts of my body as well as my hands. Years of practice later, this is now my primary method for evaluation—I begin each treatment with my fingertips on the Heart chakra, and I feel in my own body what needs treatment in my client's body—kind of like checking under the hood of a car. As I work with each chakra, I pay attention to which areas react in my own body. This gives me information for the chakra association technique.

- Take constant inventory of your body
- If one of your palms is more sensitive than the other, change your hands around
- Look for any change in sensation in your feet, legs, head or torso

Chakra Association

Sometimes, when your hands are over two different areas, the "whole" is greater than the sum of the parts. Separately, each area has a certain energetic quality, but when your hands are over both areas, one or both areas feel very different.

To identify an association, find one chakra that is out of balance while doing your usual Reiki procedures. Leaving one hand over this chakra, move the other hand, placing it over each of the other major chakras for a few moments to test if you feel a change in the first chakra. If you perceive a change, this indicates a connection of some sort between the two chakras and they may be treated together until both have the gentle sensation indicating balance.

A common association for women exists between the Sacral and 3rd Eye chakras. At the physical level, it is a connection between the pituitary gland and the reproductive organs. When I notice this connection, I ask my client if she has any issues with hormonal imbalance. The answer is almost always yes—either PMS, menopause, or something related. I mentioned this to Lao Xie and he added that this connection is also about fear (for men too). It is a relationship between the change and adaptability experiences which reside in the Sacral chakra and the monkey mind of the 3rd Eye chakra, and might indicate an unhealthy fear or resistance to change.

Another common connection exists between the Solar Plexus, 3rd Eye and Crown chakras. The Solar Plexus and 3rd Eye combination might indicate diabetes at the physical level (pituitary and Pancreas). At the emotional level, your client might be living an experience in which she is suffering because people don't agree with her or respect her opinions. In addition, this can be the pride of the Solar Plexus interacting with the intellect of the mind and the divine humility of the Crown).

Sometimes we don't know what the association means. One of my clients had begun experiencing intense pain in the tips of her fingers. This association technique revealed a connection between the fingers and the Throat chakra. Later she was diagnosed with herniated discs in the neck.

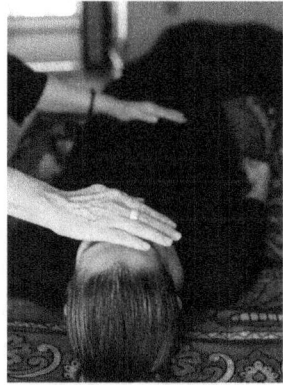 

3rd Eye/Sacral   3rd Eye/Crown/SP

Unblocking Difficult Chakras

A cool feeling (when you usually feel warmth or vibration) or no sensation at all indicates a blockage of energy. If your treatment of the chakra (or chakras, if using the chakra association technique) doesn't resolve the blockage, try one of the following techniques:

- Treat the Yong Quan—many times difficult chakras will open after you treat the Yong Quan (soles of the feet).

- Use Entrainment—influence the blocked chakra (by treating it with the right hand) with a chakra that is flowing well (by touching it with the left hand). This technique mimics phenomena found in the physical world, and here are three examples. Plucking the G-string of one guitar will elicit vibration and sound from the G-string of a nearby guitar. If the pendulums of several clocks in the same room are each swinging at different times, eventually they will all swing together. If a group of women lives together, such as in a college dormitory, they eventually tend to each have their menstrual periods at about the same time of the month.

I have actually used my own chakras to entrain my clients' chakras, but not very often.

Assessing Overall Energetic Health

The flow of energy at the Yong Quan has become my most direct indication of overall energetic health. After I told my friend who is a Master Clinical Aromatherapist my Yong Quan stories, she said that in Aromatherapy the Yong Quan is known as the Spring of Life. I have only found the Yong Quan to be blocked twice—when the major chakras were slightly depleted, but not blocked, and also Reiki did not clear the blockage. These two people were both very close to death. One I knew about, as she was in stage 4 breast cancer which had spread to her brain. The other I didn't know about—this young woman came in complaining of a severe lack of energy; she suffered a heart attack later in the week caused by almost complete blockage of blood flow, but was treated with balloon angioplasty and recovered.

Also, pay close attention to a *change* in the feel of the aura—this is useful for returning clients. A feeling that the aura shrank, or contracted—you must hold your hands much closer to the body than in previous treatments in order to sense it—is a sign of declining health or extreme fearfulness. Another sign is that the aura feels softer than in previous treatments. Some people's auras always feel soft—remember it's the change you're looking for.

As far as talking about these things with your client, be compassionate and subtle. Use your judgment on what to communicate as you might not be interpreting the feel of energy correctly—you might be wrong. If your client has a terminal condition which they know about, there's probably no need for any communication. If you sense that your client is very ill and not aware of it, you could subtly suggest they see a doctor. In all of these circumstances, offer to work with her on emotional integration.

Mahaananda Reiki Master Level

Master Level Spiritual Techniques

KamaChakra

KamaChakra is a Sanskrit term meaning "Perpetual Movement of Desire". This process assists us in purifying desire—dissolving not the desire, but the *suffering* of desire. Desire is the most difficult suffering to resolve (other than survival issues), because it resides deep within the cells of our bodies.

Desire isn't evil—God gave us yearning (desire) and pleasure which satisfies that yearning in order to ensure survival of the species. At the deepest level, our genetic code causes physical attraction to others and the drive to have sex and orgasm, resulting in children. Desire expresses itself at the emotional level; we feel separation and the need to be with others, and we fall in love. At the mental level, we are attracted to personality traits and similar interests, feeling affection and enjoying the company of others. We will experience desire while we exist in a human body—it is the will of God.

Why does this perfect divine plan cause so much suffering? It's not the desire itself, but rather our attachments and expectations about relationships and our socially programmed habit of pushing down and hiding all of this inside ourselves which causes suffering. Here are some common causes of suffering—I've experienced most of them, how about you?

- The person you desire is not available for you (doesn't know you exist, doesn't love you back, or is in a relationship)
- You don't express your desires because of guilt, or fear of rejection
- You don't act on your desires because you choose to be loyal or responsible
- You feel guilty about your desires, whether you fulfill them or not
- You hide your desires from others and yourself
- You judge the choices that other people make

To master desire, practice at experiencing it from an enlightened point of view. Begin by accepting (or at least contemplating) that at the level of Soul you (and others) are genetically, emotionally, and mentally built to experience love in every way, free of any social restrictions— *to be in love with everything, or to be in a state of Love*. This is not permission to act irresponsibly; it's freedom to let go of judgment.

Next, actively work towards *unattaching from the person you desire*. Non-attachment doesn't mean to get rid of something; it doesn't mean you won't experience the feel of desire any more, or that you have to push away the person you desire. Non-attachment means fully enjoying someone or something while you are having the experience, and at the same time fully accepting that everything is impermanent. If you can master non-attachment, the pain of an ended relationship will be much less intense, or it won't last very long.

Practice at becoming fully aware of the natural forces inside yourself. *Your desires are reactions in your body; you are not your desires.* Consciously observe them with compassion for yourself, and without drama. It won't feel so much like "I can't have what I want, and I'm not happy", but more like "Oh, I'm aware that my body is yearning for something". From this perception, you can dissolve the suffering with emotional integration.

The First Mantra of Kama Chakra

Maha created the Kama Chakra process with 10 mantras. The entire process guides you to transform your perception of desire from human suffering to spiritual joy. Mahaananda Reiki focuses on the first mantra*, as its consciousness is synchronistic with Reiki—it helps to relax resistance to evolution. The Mahaananda Reiki Master initiation process includes this mantra.

The first mantra of Kama Chakra brings you peace and compassion with your physical, emotional and mental desires. The first step in mastering desire is to let go of resisting them, and of feeling like a victim because of them.

"Om Dhim Klim Hrim
Shanti Karuna Kama"

Om	"ohm"	Universal syllable
Dhim	"deem"	Physical substance
Klim	"kleem"	Desires and feelings
Hrim	"hreem"	Purification
Shanti	"*shahn*-tee"	Peace
Karuna	"kah-*roo*-nah"	Compassion
Kama	"*kah*-mah"	Desires

Recite one mala per day for 41 days (or 45 minutes per day) while gazing steadily at the Sri Yantra (see below), imagining yourself inside the womb of Divine Mother. Do emotional integration every day after your mantras. After completing the charging process, you can recite one mala at each full moon (this can be done the day before, the day of, or the day after the full moon).

*For instruction in the entire Kama Chakra process, contact the ShaktiMa organization at info@shaktima.org.

The Sri Yantra of Divine Mother

Sri Yantra ("shree *yahn*-trah") means Supreme Tool and represents the womb of Divine Mother.

(You can find the color version of the Sri Yantra at www.desertlotusreikiandmeditation.com.)

The Unbreakable Gaze

Do you remember as a child hearing about (or even conducting) the experiment of killing an ant with a magnifying glass? Sunlight warms an ant, but directing it on the ant with the magnifying glass so focuses that warmth that it creates a powerful transformation—it burns up the ant. The following techniques will strengthen your focus, creating more powerful transformations in your therapy (however, these techniques bring powerful benefits rather than powerful destruction).

- The Yeouan Technique incarnates your soul
- Fixity quiets your mental noise
- The Five Breath Meditation gently pulls you into the present moment

The YEOUAN Technique

The YEOUAN "*yoh*-wahn" technique, a Kabbalistic meditation, activates your chakras and incarnates Soul and consciousness. For most of us, in our normal non-meditative state only about 2% of the soul resides in the body. Up to about 10% of the soul resides in the bodies of highly evolved beings. Incarnating soul means bringing more of your soul into your body—it raises your consciousness, and therefore your therapy power.

The practice consists of toning each of the five Hebrew vowels as you contemplate a state of being and the chakra in which it resonates. See the end of this section for the guidelines on charging the vowels.

<u>Toning and Contemplation</u>

To tone a vowel, sing it on one steady pitch for 20 minutes, loud enough to feel the vibration in your chakra. Continue each tone just until you begin to feel uncomfortable from lack of air, then take a normal breath and continue. If you are not alone, you may tone silently.

- **I** This vowel is pronounced like the "ee" in the word "keep". The meaning of I is intention at the highest level of pure thought—without attachment, expectation or judgment. Pay attention to your 3rd Eye chakra, contemplate the meaning, and tone.

- **E** This vowel is pronounced like the "a" in the word "play". The meaning of E is wisdom—what we learn as a result of experience. Pay attention to your Throat chakra, contemplate the meaning, and tone.

- **O** This vowel is pronounced like the "o" in the word "hope". The meaning of O is everything—from your own self-containment to the entire universe, in a state of Oneness. Pay attention to your Heart chakra, contemplate the meaning, and tone.

- **U** This vowel is pronounced like the "u" in the word "tune". The meaning of U is experience--to exist and to feel. Pay attention to your Solar Plexus chakra, contemplate the meaning, and tone.

- **A** This vowel is pronounced like the "au" in the word "autumn". The meaning of A is presence—being here and now in self-awareness. Pay attention to your entire abdomen, contemplate the meaning, and tone.

- **N,** pronounced "nnnnn". Become aware of the physical feel of your body from the inside. Pay attention to either the Base chakra or your entire body. This consonant is not toned alone, but along with the vowels (see below). This brings each of the states of being of the vowels into your physical body as one unified state of being.

<u>Charging the Hebrew Vowels</u>

The incarnation of the consciousness of the vowels is a 10-day process. Pay attention to the chakra, contemplate the meaning, and tone the vowel as follows:

- Day 1: do the process with "I" continuously for 20 minutes
- Day 2: do the process with "E" continuously for 20 minutes
- Day 3: do the process with "O" continuously for 20 minutes
- Day 4: do the process with "U" continuously for 20 minutes
- Day 5: do the process with "A" continuously for 20 minutes
- Day 6: tone all vowels one after another in one breath, adding an elongated "N" at the end continuously for 20 minutes. "I-E-O-U-A-Nnnnnnnn".
- Day 7: (same as Day 6)
- Day 8: (same as Day 6)
- Day 9: (same as Day 6)
- Day 10: (same as Day 6)

Fixity Meditation

Fixity is gazing at a point ("fixing" it with your eyes) without really looking at it, and keeping your conscious attention on that point. The goal of fixity meditation is to clear your mind of thoughts as you allow a powerful focused attention to a single point. You will use three simple tools to develop this skill: sitting, looking and breathing.

Preparation

Find the point you want to fix—it should be directly in front of you, a few feet lower than eye level. For example, a spot on the carpet if you are sitting on the floor, or a spot on a blank wall if you are sitting on a chair. I've used a freckle on my knee while sitting cross-legged. You might review the section on What is Meditation for a reminder on how to unattach from your thoughts. It can also be helpful to do some gentle physical movement just before your meditation, such as walking, yoga or Tai Chi.

- Sit—and get everything out of your system. Scratch what itches, rub your eyes, stretch your body, have a drink of water, blow your nose...then take a few deep breaths and consciously relax your muscles.

- Look—pay attention to your spot and fix it with an unfocused gaze. The best results come from fixing your spot while at the same time being conscious of yourself—being aware that you are aware of yourself. Do your best to pay no attention to thoughts—neither words nor images.

- Breathe—pay attention to your breathing to help you focus on your spot.

Fixity Experiences

If your experience is similar to mine, your thoughts will bombard you at first—this is normal, as your mind is throwing out the trash. Then thoughts will come in waves. My eyes might jump around my spot, refusing to settle on it. If this happens, gently allow your thoughts to fade into the background. Every time you notice that you are thinking, softly bring yourself back. And some days are just better than others, accept it.

Emotions will rise. When my practice is difficult, I feel shame and the victim-ness of self-persecution in my abdomen. I can spend a good chunk of my fixity practice doing integration about all this. Even if you feel that your practice is not successful because your mind won't settle, know that your time is well spent. Because you remain in practice disregarding what you would prefer to do, and because you integrate your emotions, you are mastering your ego. Don't judge yourself.

It will eventually become more common that fixity goes well for you and your mind is relatively quiet. Sometimes what I am gazing at on the carpet or the wall seems to move in slow breaths or waves—it can resemble the swells of the ocean, or move in spirals. I also transcend, sometimes consciously and sometimes not (refer back to the discussion of transcendence in the "What is Meditation" section).

<u>Practicing Fixity</u>

Practice fixity with your eyes open, using no mantra, 5 days in a row for 20 minutes. Then move on to practice for 1 hour, for 5 days in a row.

The Five Breath Meditation

This meditation comes from Thich Nhat Hanh's book "The Miracle of Mindfulness: An Introduction to the Practice of Meditation". Thich Nhat Hanh is a Vietnamese Buddhist monk and peace activist. Maha and this modern-day Zen master were both delegates to the 2008 United Nations Day of Vesak in Hanoi, Vietnam, which addressed the spiritual, academic, cultural and religious aspects of Buddhism.

The Five Breath meditation helps you relax into the present moment, in the here and the now. In the present moment, you can let go of your fear and worry about the future. You can let go of your anger, grief and regrets about the past. Your natural state is simple happiness, and existing in the present moment allows you to relax into it. You let go of the drama of attachment and expectation, in a pure state that brings power to therapy.

The technique involves a series of five breaths, and you will think a particular thought with each of your inhales and exhales. Breathe softly and deeply throughout the process, except for each "2nd" breath—here you inhale vigorously, followed by a soft exhale. And when you think "I smile" during the fourth inhale, really smile! (and force yourself if you don't feel like it). Do your best to feel the words you are thinking, and pay attention to your breath all along.

Inhale	Exhale
I inhale,	I exhale
Deeper,	More gentle
I am calm,	I relax
I smile ☺,	I am free
Present moment,	Wonderful moment

This just might be the easiest meditation in this book, and it's pretty much guaranteed to make you feel light and happy. It's definitely a favorite of my beginning meditation students.

Perform this technique continuously for 20 minutes per day, for nine consecutive days.

Divine and Universal Consciousness of the Chakra

Lao Xie said that the word universe means One Song (uni-verse). "Universal" is not only what exists in every direction, it is also what exists at every level of vibration.

In Level I you contemplated the chakra as a constantly turning subtle center of vital energy which draws universal life force energy into and through the body, affecting physical, emotional and mental health. You went deeper in Level II, contemplating that each chakra is a sensory organ of the soul which tastes the human experience and provides evolutionary lessons. Both the human and soul perspectives are local perceptions (from one point of view); now we'll contemplate chakras from the universal perspective.

The turning, or resonance, of the chakra arises from the perfection and apparent dichotomy of existing as both human and divine at the same time. In the beginning, God existed as Void, but wanted to experience Love. Because this experience requires interaction, God generated a great force of separation (also known scientifically as the Big Bang) and pushed Himself into the world. Part of this push created souls—each one is fully and completely God but from its own unique point of view. This is like raindrops falling from a cloud. And soul/God incarnates itself in physical form and lives the human experience, allowing God to have every possible experience of Love.

God desires to be incarnate in the tangible world (separation), and yet the soul yearns for Oneness with God again (love). From the most subtle waves of energy to the highest level of the cosmos, there is love and separation. The interaction of these forces of divine attraction and repulsion result in consciousness turning on itself—this is the turning of the chakra.

Each chakra is a manifestation of universal consciousness, and although this consciousness may seem to exist locally in one area of one human body, there is the one chakra which exists everywhere. It is universal convection, or the VishwaChakra. To sink deeply into the experience of just one of your chakras is to fall into the immensity of the universe. As Above, So Below. The movement and expansion of supreme consciousness—from the highest level of the cosmos, to the chakra, to the smallest vibration of energy waves in an atom—is the same. The following guided meditation takes your attention through each of the chakras, and then all at the same time, until finally you feel the VishwaChakra inside you and everywhere.

Meditation on the VishwaChakra

Breathe, relax, and clear your mind. As you breathe, feel the breath move through your nose, and notice the rise and fall of your abdomen. Place attention inside your body. If your mind is moving, pay attention to your breathing or do a few recitations of the Peace mantra.

Pay attention to the sensation of vital energy in your entire body. You may feel a subtle vibration or warmth.

Pay attention to the Crown chakra...when you feel the vibration of the chi, stay there a while and experience it...

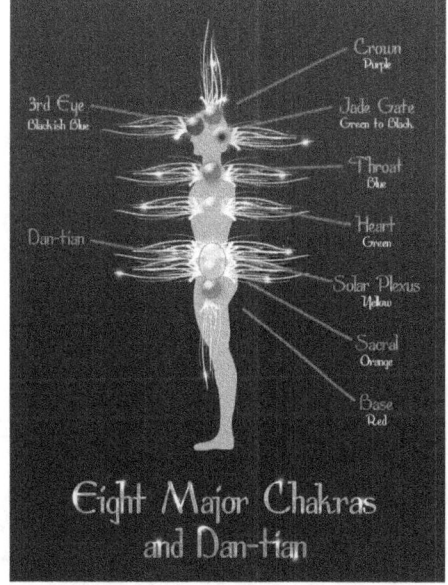

Now, move your attention to the Third Eye and spend some time...

Now, focus on the Jade Gate and sit there...

Now, become aware of the Throat ...

Now, the Heart...

Now, the Solar Plexus...

Now, the Dan-Tian...

Now, the Sacral chakra...

Now, the Base chakra...

Return to the Heart chakra, place your attention there, and sink into it...

Keeping your attention in the Heart, also add your awareness one at a time to each of the other chakras. It is an unfocused gaze, to feel all of them at once. Observe the Crown...add the Third Eye...and the Jade Gate...and the Throat...and the Solar Plexus...and the Dan-Tian...and the Sacral...and the Base...The awareness of the vibration intensifies.

You are experiencing all the chakras at once, while living in the Heart. What seems to distinguish each of them begins to fade and dissolve. There is only one chakra in your body, and the Cosmos is consumed in this chakra. Release resistance and sink into the resonance of your energy. Allow yourself to fall into the immensity of the universe...the vibration of you is the vibration of the cosmos.

Mahaananda Mantra

The Mahaananda mantra invokes the consciousness of the Mahaananda therapist—it is the Gaze of the Soul. The mantra brings you to know yourself as divine (Mahaananda), soul (Aadyaatmika) and human (Svabhaavaya), all as one unified experience. Then you can be aware of living in all three of these worlds at the same time.

"Om Namah Mahaananda Aadyaatmika Svabhaavaya Hum"

Om	"ohm"	Universal syllable
Namah	"nuhm-*ah*"	Acknowledge or commune with
Mahaananda	"mah-hah-*nahn*-dah"	Great bliss
Aadyaatmika	"ah-deeyaht-*mee*-kah"	Spiritual one (pure one who uses the Self)
Svabhaavaya	"svah-bah-*vie*-yuh"	Created from Truth (what is inherent in nature)
Hum	"hoom"	Bija mantra of experience

- Mahaananda—you are part of God's expression of Himself in the world, which is Bliss. You are divine incarnation.
- Aadyaatmika—your soul observes what causes happiness and suffering at the level of your human life. The only possible result is evolution.
- Svabhaavaya—you live life and feel your physical body's reactions to your experiences—happiness and suffering

Sit quietly for 15 minutes a day for 3 days. Briefly contemplate each of these three concepts as what you (and your clients) are made of. Ask yourself "Who Am I?" and for the remainder of your meditation time softly pay attention inside, without looking for an answer. This meditation elevates your perception of yourself, and as a side effect it will also help you become more aware of energies and the effects produced by your Reiki therapy.

Charge the mantra by chanting 9 malas a day for 12 days.

The Vajra State of Being

The Master Teacher embodies and shares the consciousness of the Vajra during the initiation ritual.

The dictionary definition of the Sanskrit word "Vajra" is lightning bolt or diamond. And because of the inherent properties of the lightning bolt (ungraspable, irresistible force) and the diamond (indestructibility), "Vajra" is used to represent the soul in Hindu and Buddhist prayers. It also refers to the ritual object we use in meditation. You can find a Vajra in a Buddhist shop or on Amazon.

Sigung taught that the Vajra represents both the Three Centers (man) and the Three Worlds (man's relationship to the universe). An energy field surrounds each of your three centers; with movement (Qigong) and passive meditation, these energy fields expand into the unified field. The larger your energy fields grow, the greater the potential transformation—in this way, your Reiki therapy becomes more powerful. In the Three Worlds, Heaven and Earth meet in your Heart chakra or Dan-Tian. I once heard Lao Xie say that your hands do the work of your heart; so energy flows from heaven and earth into your heart, then out through your hands. He also said that if we try to hold onto the energy that we gather, we'll get sick—we must let it flow out. Sigung taught that enlightenment is the ability to live in all Three Worlds simultaneously (the same concept as the Mahaananda mantra.)

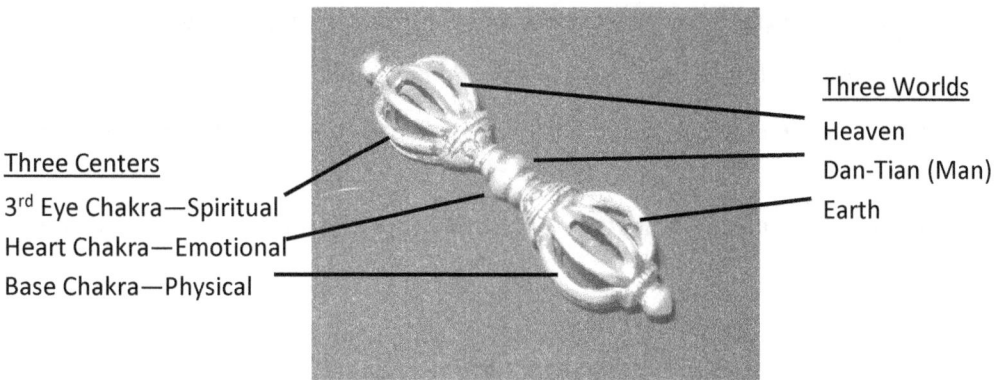

Three Centers
3rd Eye Chakra—Spiritual
Heart Chakra—Emotional
Base Chakra—Physical

Three Worlds
Heaven
Dan-Tian (Man)
Earth

In nature, great pressure applied to the common substance of coal creates a diamond. Maha teaches that emotional integration and spiritual practice (the pressure you apply to yourself) will create the wisdom of this Vajra state of being inside you.

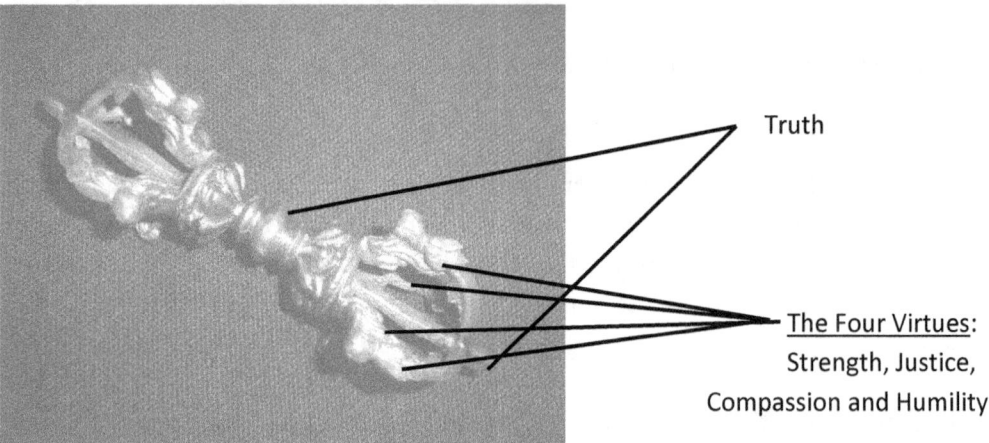

The orb at the center of the Vajra, which also extends through the entire Vajra, exemplifies the virtue of Truth. Flowing from Truth is consciousness in the form of two lotuses. The four prongs at each end of the Vajra represent the Four Virtues, which originate from consciousness; they come together as one, in Truth, at each tip of the Vajra. Once you embody the Four Virtues, you become One in Truth.

The Four Virtues and Truth represent the consciousness of the five Dhyani Buddhas:

- Amitabha, the red Buddha of Infinite Light, symbolizes Strength
- Amogasiddha, the green Almighty Conqueror or Lord of Karma, characterizes Justice
- Akshobya, the blue Unmovable Unshakable Buddha, epitomizes Compassion
- Ratnasambhava, the yellow Source of Precious Things or Jewel-Born One, exemplifies Humility
- Vairocana, the white Buddha Supreme and Eternal, the Radiant One, represents Truth

Empowering the Vajra

Empowering the Vajra raises the consciousness of Truth in your body, and also transforms your Vajra into a power item (like Japa transforms a mala).

Hold the Vajra in your right hand as shown below. The thumb represents earth, generation and protection. The major finger represents consciousness—being aware that you are aware of yourself; and heaven—where God exists all evolution happens. The ring finger represents Divine Mother—the feminine aspect of God. These three fingers touch Truth (see below).

Meditate on each Buddha for five days, fifteen minutes per day. Contemplate only one Buddha at a time, in the order listed above. The process will last 25 days.

I did this by sitting on the floor and imagining each Buddha sitting facing me. For example, when contemplating the virtue of Strength, a completely red Buddha was sitting facing me. I transmigrated into the Buddha and allowed my perception to shift to that of the red Buddha. From the point of view of the Buddha, I contemplated "What is strength?" And so on for each Buddha.

- Strength refers to the strength to remain conscious, not falling into anger.
- Justice refers to individual karma, and also equity for all from a global point of view—the concept of "fairness" resulting from comparison of one's situation to that of another fades away.
- Compassion expresses the complete understanding of suffering
- Humility remembers that all power flows from God
- Truth expresses the wisdom born from the conscious experience of the collective states of being of Strength, Justice, Compassion and Humility.

Mastering Compassion

The Compassionate Servant

You, as a Mahaananda Reiki Master, must strive to be a master of compassion. Lao Xie defines compassion as skillful and appropriate action; it is giving unconditionally with an open heart. But it is giving what is needed—what is best for others as well as for ourselves.

In the process of exploring the teachings in this book, you raise your own consciousness and become aware of how it affects your client. You use the efficiency of reciting mantras before and during treatment to move into a state of being, which then affects your client. Like traditional Reiki, your therapy is the most powerful when you let go of any control—when you let go of expectation and attachment to the outcome. How do you let go of your natural desire to "fix" the emotional or physical well-being of your client?

Begin by being mindful of the natural workings of karma. We usually accept that our souls make available certain experiences for us in this lifetime in order to learn lessons required for spiritual evolution. For therapists, respecting this same karma (or God's will) for others is a lot harder to accept! Contemplate that an illness is an evolutionary experience shared by the one who is ill, and by the husband, children, parents, friends, work associates, doctors, and the holistic therapist of this person—it is one flow of consciousness.

Next, be mindful of yourself. Wanting to fix everybody is a state of being of compassionate servant. Yes, but the therapist here can also play the role of the savior opposite the victim role of their clients (see the section on the 21 Masks of the Ego). If you are attached to the outcome of the Reiki treatment, you feel good when the person you helped is grateful to you (you are loved!), but you are disappointed when the treatment didn't seem to be effective (you are rejected). You might also project these judgments on yourself whether or not your client does, creating a circle of savior, self-persecution and victim. The solution is to constantly observe yourself and integrate when you become aware of it; also, to practice at being self-contained so that the perceived love (or lack of it) of others doesn't affect you (see the following section on Swaasthya).

As a true compassionate servant, do your best to trust that the experience of others is God's will for their evolution. And then, in a state of compassion, perform acts of loving kindness with no expectation or attachment to the outcome. Next are several practices which will help you get to this state of being.

Swaasthya

Swaasthya ("*swahs*-tee-yuh") is a siddhi meditation of self-containment; it will help you master the "savior" inside you. The Sanskrit dictionary defines Swaasthya as self-dependence, self-contentment, satisfaction, and comfort. Practice Swaasthya to break your emotional enslavement to the outside world.

Spend a few moments in contemplation. Your only goal is to be inside you with yourself. Drink in the nourishment and flavor of seclusion and calm. Remember you are God's expression of Himself in the world; therefore, you are made of Love. All the love and comfort you need are here inside you. Become aware of the self-sufficiency, self-love, contentment and happiness that you find while being alone with yourself (if you don't find it at first, force yourself to imagine it). Pay attention to it, allow it, become familiar with it—and sit in that state of being. Your ego's resistance to simple happiness might cause disagreeing emotions to rise. If this happens, do your emotional integration and then go back to your meditation.

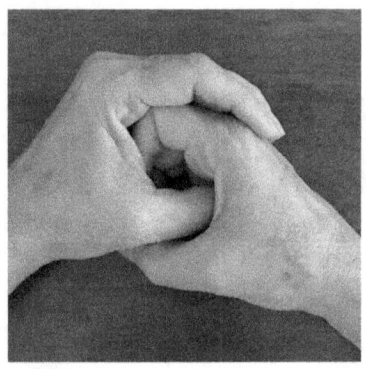

Use the Swaasthya mudra (hand position) which resembles the yin-yang symbol while meditating: Place the tip of your left thumb in the center of your right palm. Join the tips of the right thumb and right ring finger, loosely wrapping your right hand around the left thumb. Rest the fingers of your left hand on the top of the right hand.

The effect of siddhi meditation is like placing a tea bag in hot water—the feeling of it will softly permeate throughout you. The technique for this siddhi meditation is the same one you use with the first two siddhis. Place your hands in the mudra. Begin your meditation with breathing, paying attention inside, calming the mind, and observing that you are aware of yourself. Softly and slowly repeat "Swaasthya", eventually thinking it silently, while contemplating the meaning. After a few minutes, let go of the philosophical contemplation, and remain in a state of awareness while you repeat the mantra. Just be available for discovery without asking a question—a question is too active. Come back to the mental contemplation only if you notice that your mind is wandering, and then let go again.

Do this meditation for about 20 minutes per day, for a period of 33 days. Then you can meditate on Swaasthya for a few minutes before doing treatments or initiations.

Affirmation of the Compassionate Servant

This affirmation reminds you that emotion is an expression of your human experience, which you surrender just for the moment in order to do therapy at the level of soul. Humility acknowledges that all power flows from God—it is not your own, so you let go of the attachment and expectations for the outcome of your therapy. Recite the affirmation below and embrace this state of being before doing treatments or initiations.

"I offer my emotions to the Supreme Consciousness. May I be a humble servant, so that my actions are performed without attachment and without expectation. My gaze is love, my words are compassion, and my actions are respectful."

The Favorable Mantra

The Favorable mantra is more of an astrological blessing or spell than a prayer—notice that it does not begin with "Om". Use this mantra to bless the path of others for whom you provide treatment or initiation. Do it over your client at the very end of a therapy session.

Here we acknowledge the energy of the planets as they exert natural forces on each other and move perfectly in the solar system. And when they come together in certain configurations, they influence our human experience (probably almost everyone has heard of "Mercury Retrograde"). This mantra invokes the influence of the planets to help you or your client reach your goals.

"Sarvatha Kalyanam Mangala Bhavantu"

Sarvatha	"sahr-vah-*tah*"	All that is
Kalyanam	"kah-lee-ah-*nahm*"	Eternity
Mangala	"*mahng*-gah-lah"	Favorable
Bhavantu	"bah-*vahn*-too"	Generated here and now

The general meaning is "May all be eternally favorable beginning right now". The mantra requests pleasant experiences from the human point of view, but also invokes karmic experiences that are required for enlightenment—in a way that feels positive. So we are asking for a unified experience of improved human circumstances and non-resistance to the soul lesson.

Charge this mantra with the 9 x 12 formula, holding your left palm open and up to receive energy from the planets; this keeps you from using your own energy with the blessing.

While giving the blessing, hold your left hand up toward the planets, and place your right hand on or over your client where it feels best to you. I usually place it above or facing the 3rd Eye or Heart chakra. Do this in your mind if you think your client might be disturbed by the process.

Divine Mother / VishwaShakti

Just as important as having compassion for others is having compassion for yourself. When you practice of Mahaananda Reiki, you to face suffering often. Eventually you won't find much difference between your own suffering and the suffering of your clients; simply, there is suffering. *You must care for yourself in order to lighten the weight of this experience; otherwise you could jeopardize your physical and emotional health.* Now you have many techniques to help you do this, such as practicing emotional integration, reciting mantras for yourself, passive meditation and contemplation. And Divine Mother, or Shakti, is there for you.

Shakti, the feminine energies and aspect of God, exists everywhere (Vishwa). She is the substance of the universe—everything is made of Shakti. She is the womb of the world, caring for creation in every moment and in every detail; and creation includes the unified consciousness of *your* human, soul and divine universal experience.

Shakti supports you in your evolution and in your therapy. She doesn't provoke your evolution; she simply supports it gently with kindness and a non-judgmental and forgiving love. Although her power is immense enough to support the world, she is cooling, soothing and nurturing, and feels of subtle softness. She helps you soften your attachments, which allows you to flow more easily from experience to experience, all according to the will of God. To discover this, contemplate the Five Elements and the consciousness of water, which represents Divine Mother.

Jesus' mother Mary is an embodiment of Divine Mother. Consider a universal meaning of the phrase in the Hail Mary prayer "pray for us sinners, now and at the hour of our death". "Sinners" refers to our state of being of suffering, and "Death" refers to every painful time we master an emotion and evolve—we invoke the consciousness of Divine Mother as we move from one experience to the next.

Contemplate this teaching with the goal of surrendering yourself into the care of Shakti, and opening yourself to receive the Grace she bestows.

Consciousness of Usui Sensei

As I mentioned in the Lineage section, Maha received initiation and wisdom transmission directly from Usui Sensei through soul level communion. This powerful and lovely experience in the consciousness of Usui Sensei can be understood only when you are far along in the Mahaananda path. It will be shared as part of your **Mahaananda Reiki Master Teacher initiation** if you choose to receive that training.

Master Level Reiki

Fourth Reiki Symbol—Dai Ko Myo

(Pronounced "die-koh-*myoh*")

Most Reiki-ists interpret the Great Light Radiance as the ability for light to shine through you; however, the deeper meaning refers to your own enlightened nature that radiates to others. Once spirit (Rei 霊) masters the mind or inner nature (Ki 気), one reaches enlightenment.

Kanji (*information for interpretation only—use the symbol above for initiation*):

Dai:	大	Great
Ko:	光	Light
Myo:	明	Radiance

This fourth symbol is stylized, especially the last kanji.

Practical Applications of Dai Ko Myo

Dai Ko Myo is the Master Symbol—the common meanings are Mastership, Empowerment, or The One with the Mahayana Heart of Giving (from Lao Xie). Mahayana Buddhism, which mean the Great Vehicle, is a spiritual practice done with the intent to help both yourself and others.

The Reiki Master Teacher uses Dai Ko Myo to initiate Reiki Masters.

Additional Techniques

Sigung taught the following techniques, most of which incorporate concepts from the martial arts. At the master level, you are free to use what you love and have personally experienced (such as crystals).

Unblocking Difficult Chakras

<u>Tap</u> Lightly tap on the chakra (gently touching the body except for the Base chakra) with your index and middle fingers—the sword charm mudra described in the teaching on Symbol Empowerment—to open this chakra with additional vibration.

<u>Vibrating Palm</u> With your right hand a few inches from your client's body, palm facing the chakra and fingers slightly apart and relaxed, vibrate the palm of your hand to create a more powerful emanation of chi. Perfect the technique this way prior to applying it: with the palm facing down, swivel the palm like the common hand movement we use to indicate "more or less". In my hometown, we say it in Spanish, "mas o menos". Practice until you can do it rapidly and with very little movement; you could visualize your hand on a jackhammer. Try it out on yourself by giving hands-off Reiki to your 3rd Eye with your right hand; then begin to use vibrating palm to experience the difference.

<u>Extraction</u> Pull out the blockage with your left hand (like a weed), and cut the "roots" with your right hand in the sword charm mudra. Place the blockage in the earth for purification. Sometimes I use a counter-clockwise circular motion with my scanning hand to draw out the blockage first.

<u>Loosen</u> Stagnant energy may seem to block the chakra. Use Raku with your hand in the sword charm mudra to "shock" and loosen the attachment of the blockage. Raku is a lightning bolt—a powerful non-Reiki symbol—found in the teaching on Symbol Empowerment. You may also use your sword mudra to mimic a sword cut to slice open the stagnant energy.

Other Techniques

<u>Iron Palm Qigong</u> Scan the body of your client, beginning with both hands at the Heart chakra and sliding them apart—one hand will slide to the Crown, the other to the Base. You are looking for disturbances which identify the source of pain. This may feel like ripples of water when a pebble drops into a lake. Now hold your hands side by side over the area of disturbed

chi. Your left hand remains at the same height, but your right hand moves up and down, with the wrist leading the movement like painting a wall with a paint brush. Do this until you no longer feel the blockage through the right hand. Your right hand transmits cleansing Reiki while your left hand receives negative energy that is flushed out. Finally, lower your left hand toward the ground and release the negative energy into the earth for purification.

Adding Intent   After you have scanned the body and identified a chakra which needs treatment, place both of your hands over the chakra, and feel and say to yourself "physical", then "emotional", then "chemical", then "spiritual". If any of these expressions creates an energetic response in the chakra, add the following intent to your treatment: for "physical" add "relax"; for "emotional" add "release"; for "chemical" add "balance" or "purify"; and if "spiritual" add "ascend". This example assumes you used your palms to scan and identify the chakra that needs treatment. You can do this with any scanning method, such as a pendulum—identify the unbalanced chakra with the pendulum, then use the pendulum at that chakra while you ask the question "physical, emotional, chemical or spiritual". This works well with muscle testing also.

Ascended Masters   Some people are aware of a presence or feeling of other beings in attendance during a therapy session, and it is commonly called "Ascended Masters". Whether or not you experience this awareness, you may humbly request assistance. Humility doesn't mean feeling small or insignificant—it is the feeling that you are a tool through which the will of God flows. As God brings you to find your teachers, you in turn will use their consciousness as a tool also. I often feel the presence of Usui Sensei, Sigung, Maha and Lao Xie (some are ascended, others aren't)—if I don't feel them, I don't hesitate to ask for them. I also always ask for assistance from Jesus and Divine Mother.

In my experience, assistance comes in several forms—the feeling of powerful consciousness; intuitive understanding of emotional state of being; intuition for hand positions; increased flow of energy in a weak chakra; and experience by both me and my client that there are more people in the room, or more hands on the body, than just me. Be sure to feel gratitude along with your humility.

Conclusion

This practice has deeply blessed my spiritual evolution and enhanced my therapeutic abilities. The wisdom will only come to you through experience—I sincerely wish that each of you can feel the blessings of my masters in this teaching, and choose to experience it for yourself.

For personal instruction on spiritual techniques included in this book, please contact me at sukhi@desertlotusreikiandmeditation.com, or the ShaktiMa organization at info@shaktima.org.

References

"Advanced Kuji-In" by Maha Vajra, F.Lepine Publishing, 2006

"Broaden Your Perception" by Simon Lacouline, F.Lepine Publishing, 2009

"Kuji-Kiri and Majutsu" by MahaVajra, F.Lepine Publishing, 2008

"The Esoteric World of Chakras" by SukhiDevi, F.Lepine Publishing, 2013

The oral teachings of MahaVajra

The oral teachings of Sigung Hasting Albo

The oral teachings of Lao Xie Christopher Lee Matsuo